Breaking free to be you after domestic violence

Stories of strength and success

Compiled by
KC Andrews

Copyright © Broken to Brilliant™

The moral right of the authors has been asserted.

First published in Australia in 2016
by Broken to Brilliant Ltd™, Brisbane, Australia

ISBN

Paperback: 978-0-9945714-0-3

Epub: 978-0-9945714-0-1

Mobi: 978-0-9945714-2-7

All rights reserved. No part of this book may be reproduced or transmitted by any person or entity (including Google, Amazon or similar organisations), in any form or by any means, electronic or mechanical, including photocopying, recording, scanning or by any information storage and retrieval system, without prior permission in writing from the publisher.

Cataloguing-in-Publication entry is available from the
National Library of Australia http://catalogue.nla.gov.au

Cover images copyright © Natalie Reid

PRAISE FOR *BROKEN TO BRILLIANT*

Broken to Brilliant is an inspiring collection of poignant stories celebrating the solidarity of shared adversity and is therefore an invaluable resource for every woman who still suffers in silence.
Kelly Niland, Educator

If you are serious about changing your life after domestic violence, read this book. It gives practical information about how you can turn your life around, by women just like you. Many of them have been subjected to the worst possible domestic violence, but from the depths of despair and/or debt have reached for the skies and grasped brilliance firmly with both hands.
Shireen, Communications Specialist

With great care and dignity, KC Andrews brings together the stories of ten inspiring women who lead us through their own journey of survival, hope, and a way forward. As human beings we search for meaning in our lives, particularly during times of conflict and suffering where we question why life has sent us the challenges before us. The journeys of these women will connect with many and provide a source of strength to each of us. I recommend this book to men and women who draw personal courage and conviction from the stories of the heroes and role models amongst us. *Tracey, Teacher*

I have always believed that there is brilliance within every person, but that sometimes we lose sight of it, or perhaps are not even aware of its existence. *Broken to Brilliant* is a collection of personal stories that will show you how the human spirit can triumph over adversity, and step into brilliance. I wholeheartedly recommend this book to anyone who is facing hard times, and feels broken. I promise you will be inspired by every story. *Dr Fiona Hawthorne PhD, Churchill Fellow, General Manager Hummingbird House*

I have attended a lot of courses and conferences and worked on my inner self, but this process of telling my story has been very therapeutic. *Author, Broken to Brilliant Chapter Five, Tears and Time*

*This isn't just another book;
it is from survivors dedicated to fellow domestic violence survivors.
May each page you turn guide you to a new chapter in your life.*

THANK YOU

To the women who shared their stories, thank you for being brave, baring your soul and being willing to help others rebuild their lives without financial gain or personal recognition. You know who you are.

This book was fuelled by a personal drive to make a difference and to share an easier way to rebuild your life after domestic violence.

To everyone who supported and encouraged the 2.5-year-long labour of love to birth the book *Broken to Brilliant,* thank you. Behind the printing press there have been so many people helping to shape this book. It has taken:

- referrals and recommendations
- financial contributions of over $5,310
- volunteer proof readers
- legal review
- publishing consultant
- cover design and photography
- logo design and marketing materials
- web publishing
- and lots of coffee and pizza!

Thank you to my children who lived through this, but pulled through stronger. You amaze me every day.

Thank you to those who provided words of encouragement. You kept the fire burning despite the many road blocks encountered.

KC Andrews

"Beautiful souls are shaped by ugly experiences."
Matshona Dhliwayo

FOREWORD

It is no easy feat to sit down, write and relive the trials contained in these women's stories for public perusal, regardless of the noble intention of them being placed together inside of a book. And yet they have done it; written about their lives, the agony and the redemption, so that other women can understand a little of how some women suffer at the hands of those they love, how they survive and, ultimately, thrive.

Instinctively we shy away from sharing our pain for fear of being misunderstood, of others diminishing the gravity and complexity of our pain or worse, of being shunned or rejected. But when we do so, it can become part of our own healing and serve as liberation for those who have experienced a similar kind of pain, but have not healed just yet. That is the beauty of this book – the gravity of being courageous when instinct tells us to run, hide and cover the darkness of our wounds with a mask that serves no-one.

It is my hope that for some readers the courage of these women's stories will be a balm amid their struggle, the catalyst for their own liberation to become a decider and survivor of their own histories and ultimately a thriver.

One woman, who was once broken and is now brilliant, has inspired and birthed this collection. She had the vision to encourage women to tell their stories, to bring in light where there has been darkness, and project it on to the collective consciousness so that we all can become more conscious of how so many of our sisters and children live behind closed doors.

When we do speak of the unspeakable individually and document it, it moves from being a collective coma of statistics about a number of unknown individuals, to a very real gash on our society's soul. Having any number of family, friends, neighbours or persons that we pass on the street be affected by domestic violence should call to the community's conscience to wake up.

Because it is not just the individuals' lives that are being affected by such trauma; it is also the lifeblood of our community that feels this trauma, whether we are conscious of the particulars or not.

This is a truly courageous book. I thank each writer for being so brave for themselves, their families and our community. For allowing us into their lives so we can learn, understand and ultimately make domestic violence part of our distant past. Truly, let the individual and communal healing begin.

Jane Monica-Jones

Jane Monica-Jones is an author, teacher, and personal development facilitator.

www.janemonicajones.com

CONTENTS

PRAISE FOR BROKEN TO BRILLIANT iii

THANK YOU vii

FOREWORD ix

INTRODUCTION 1

CHAPTER ONE
    How to Plan, Protect and Prosper 8

CHAPTER TWO
    There is Great Strength in Gentleness 23

CHAPTER THREE
    Pieces to a better life 40

CHAPTER FOUR
    Beginning with Me 54

CHAPTER FIVE
    Tears and Time 71

CHAPTER SIX
    The Badge of Suffering 83

CHAPTER SEVEN
    Genuine Human Kindness Can Change Your Life 94

CHAPTER EIGHT
    A Journey of Self-Discovery 107

CHAPTER NINE
    My Wish for Happiness 117

CHAPTER TEN
    We All Need a Slice of SPAM 133

GLOSSARY 146

CONTACT NUMBERS 149

ENDNOTES 153

INTRODUCTION

"I am too strong for that to happen to me, I would walk out!"

WHILE TRAINING AS A NURSE, I RECALL A TUTORIAL ON DOMESTIC violence. As we all sat crossed legged on the floor and discussed the case study, my response was – "I am too strong for that to happen to me, I would walk out!"

I didn't walk out. When I started thinking about writing a book, my story was focused on living with a compulsive gambler. After we both attended marriage counselling sessions, I discovered that how we had been living was not just the result of gambling. During one of those sessions, we were put into separate programs. It was then that I learned that I was really living in a domestic violence relationship.

I discovered that you can be a strong, well educated person and yet be unable to just walk out. I had held that view, "Just walk out!" and there are many people who still hold this view and judge those who stay.

It took me years to finally leave. While setting up my and my children's new life, I kept hearing an inner voice that wanted me to create a WAAVE, a wave of women **W**orking **A**gainst **A**buse, **V**iolence and **E**ntitlement. I envisioned a powerful wave of thousands of women fighting against the upsurge of the insistent belief held by some men, their families and others in society that it is justifiable and acceptable to abuse women because they deserve it. For me, there was not enough being done to counter the sense of entitlement of the perpetrator and their families. They were not being held to account.

A few years later, my anger was subsiding and my focus shifted to wanting to highlight how women and children successfully rebuilt their lives after domestic violence. This book is a result of taking action and believing there is a reason for living through the abuse.

This is not just a book; it is supporting the launch of Broken to Brilliant, a registered charity organisation where survivors mentor survivors creating positive new life chapters after domestic violence. It is a pay-it-forward model with coaching, mentoring, workshops, work experience placements, publishing and success centres.

Like my younger self, many people do not recognise domestic violence in all its forms. Often it is only considered serious when there is physical violence and visible injury. However, as you read this book you will discover that many women have lived through severe acts of violence that had negative life-long impacts on themselves and their children without receiving a single visible scratch.

Domestic and family violence is emotional, social, financial, verbal, sexual and physical abuse, where a family member dominates another. This is not a one-off event; it is a pattern of behaviour that escalates over time, slowly eroding the victim's confidence and ability to leave.[1]

More specifically, domestic violence occurs when one partner in a relationship attempts, by physical or psychological means, to dominate and control the other. It is an abuse of power within a relationship (heterosexual and homosexual) or after separation. In the large majority of cases, the offender is male and the victim female.[2][3] The National Council to Reduce Violence against Women and Children (NCRVWC) found that "a central element of domestic violence is an ongoing pattern of behaviour aimed at controlling one's partner through fear (for example: by using violent or threatening behaviour). Violent behaviour is a tactic used by the perpetrator to exercise power and control."[4]

The World Health Organisation has found that 35% of women worldwide have experienced either intimate partner violence or non-partner sexual violence in their lifetime, and 38% of murders of women are committed by an intimate partner.[5] Research from the 2012 Australian Bureau of Statistics (ABS) Personal Safety Survey and Australian Institute of Criminology found that both men and women in Australia experience substantial levels of violence. Of all Australian women aged 18 to 24 years, 23,584 reported they had experienced sexual assault in the 12 months prior to the survey. This equates to 64 sexual assaults per day, which is nearly three every hour. The survey also showed that 36% of women had experienced physical or sexual violence from someone they knew, it mainly (62%) occurred in their home and most (61%) had children in their care at the time. Over half (58%) never contacted police and one quarter (24%) never sought advice or support.[6] In Queensland, more than 64,000 incidents of domestic and family violence were reported and almost 13,000 breaches of domestic violence orders occurred in 2013.⁷ Queensland Hospital Patient Admitted data for all public and private acute hospitals in Queensland showed a 53% increase in hospital admissions for all causes, whereas admissions for domestic assault have risen by 73%.⁸

These alarming numbers will continue to climb while Australians continue to hold the views that women are partly responsible for rape if they are intoxicated; that when they say "NO", they really mean "yes"; and that men are incapable of controlling their need for sex.

Are you amazed? These are real survey results from the 2013 national survey on Australians' attitudes to violence against women.⁹

Many people are putting significant effort into campaigns and programs that promote No to violence, Say No to violence, Australia Says No, Unite to end violence, No Violence Against Women and the list goes on.

However, I question whether we are just continuing to highlight violence, and by highlighting it with billboards, taglines, t-shirts, adverts posters, brochures books and more, are we unintentionally making it acceptable, expected, or desensitising people and minimising its impact?

While everyone's heart, money and efforts are intended to help, are we putting the focus and a lot of energy onto VIOLENCE – the key act we all want to stop?

While the correlation of media violence and increased aggression is still being debated in the literature, I still wonder what would happen if we put this same amount of focus, energy, research and money onto what we want instead: healthy, happy, trusting, safe relationships that are full of love, care and respect? This is the opposite of violence, control and fear. Now we need the marketing geniuses to develop catchy taglines with believable and duplicable imagery.

Despite the statistics and efforts to curb the violence, how does this address the underlying feelings every single person experiences as a result of domestic violence: loss, worthlessness, feeling devoid of value and totally unloved? In many cases, they may believe that they have no purpose and there is not much reason to go on.

> **Respectful**
> **R**elationships
> **E**motionally
> **S**upportive
> **P**ositive
> **E**nriching
> **C**aring
> **T**ogetherness
> **F**riendship
> **U**nderstanding
> **L**ove
>
> BROKEN to Brilliant

However, small and seemingly insignificant acts of kindness can make a huge difference. You never know which statement or act of kindness will be that "one thing" that encouraged the person to live, fight and feel that they are of worth. Whatever you do, continue to support these women and children in whatever way you can. It can be coins for the hot water shower, a phone call, a card, a can of SPAM in a hamper basket or a safe place to stay. These simple acts of kindness made a significant impact on my family and on the women in this book. I ask you, what little thing can you do, this week, this month, this year to show kindness, love and support to another? Each person needs to know that someone cares that they exist.

You will see the impact of the choices these women have

made; they have been so broken by partners, husbands, family, bosses and society. They have been abused mentally, physically, emotionally, financially, psychologically and spiritually. Regardless of the type of torment, it affected every part of their life. But somehow, from somewhere, they found an inner strength, an inner voice, that helped them to break free and make choices that helped them rebuild their lives. Sometimes the motivation was their kids and sometimes it was their own survival.

Through their thick fog of fear, anxiety, betrayal, disbelief, pain, hurt, feelings of inadequacy, doubt or worthlessness, they fought through, only to battle more enemies on their journey. They fought the enemy of the strong unspoken and spoken disbelief that exudes from family, friends, colleagues, the perpetrator and the perpetrator's family.

Those battles were not enough.

Society on the surface appears to believe and support the principle that women should not be subjected to any form of violence. However, in getting out of an abusive relationship and getting support to be safe and rebuild their lives, the insidious system is the beginning of yet another battle. Inherent within the system is the intent to help, but it is embedded with more people who cause another layer of harm, from their disbelief, their blocking and the bureaucratic bungles that occur.

These women and their kids are scared, battered, exhausted, beaten, broken – but not defeated. A mere shadow of their former selves, they blaze through to rebuild their lives. The inner strength of these courageous women shines through the thick, dark, muddy, dangerous waters of abuse. I am in awe of how they are Broken to Brilliant. Their own strength, talents and perseverance shines through. Their magnificent and distinguished fight to rebuild their lives is never over. The biggest battle that lies between them and letting their inner brilliance shine is the battle of their inner voice.

This book will help women and their kids recognise, acknowledge, appreciate, validate and embody their accomplishments and rebuild successful lives. Through the stories of how women battled abuse – being broken and nearly defeated – to break through to reveal their true self, their inner brilliance. *Broken to Brilliant* will amaze you with their courage and reveal how to break through and shine, so you can be free to be you.

K C Andrews

CHAPTER ONE

HOW TO PLAN, PROTECT AND PROSPER

"It's not what you HAVE, it's what you DO that makes the DIFFERENCE."

Sixteen months after we met, I moved in with a fun, charming and super-responsible person – or so I thought. He had fought and won custody of his two small children, both under six at the time. He worked during the evening so he could care for the children during the day. He also had a baby to another partner and they continued to have an amicable relationship. What could be better? I had a responsible, loving partner and an instant, cute family.

I was working in the fitness industry and helped him to get a full-time job working in sales. Once we were living together, I discovered he smoked marijuana but it was no big deal as the smoking occurred occasionally and generally only at friends' houses. Things were going well; we both contributed equal money into the household and my boss promoted me to a management position.

Unfortunately after two years he lost his driver's license due to an accumulation of speeding offences. With that went the full-time job as a sales rep. He assured me, "I'll get another job."

True to his word, he found work: part time in a café and a commission-only selling job that was paid once a month. Being paid this way meant that when it was payday there was a pile of bills. Due to his irregular earnings, his contribution to the household became sporadic. He paid for his own fuel, cigarettes and half share of the rent although he couldn't afford to contribute more to the household to assist with food, electricity and phone. He assured me he would pay me back.

Due to his new work schedule he spent more time hanging around the house, and smoked marijuana at least once a week. We were also having a lot of trouble with one child, who was being disruptive at school and displayed continual problems at home: lying, throwing tantrums and stealing. Even though we had been to a number of health professionals, we were unable to find anything that offered any real help for the child's behaviour. We felt we couldn't seem to get anywhere in the big city and that relocation might provide the chance to get ahead. It would give us the change we were looking for, the chance of a better job for him, a change of schools, new acquaintances, and a fresh start.

After much deliberation I was able to get a transfer and we moved to a small town. Work was a little harder to find and he didn't know what he wanted to do. As an alternative, he decided to undertake a mature-age building apprenticeship, and though it paid poorly for the first couple of years, he was excited about this new direction. He said I needed to be prepared to be the major breadwinner for a few more years and take most of the financial responsibility in supporting the family.

He felt mixing with the tradies was great and he got on very well with everyone. There was a downside however: with these newfound friends his marijuana use increased to a couple of times a week, generally at a friend's house, though sometimes also at ours. When I raised my concerns about this, his response was, "You're too straight. You need to loosen up." His moods started fluctuating more. I put this down to life stresses, a combination of less money, our struggle with one child's continuing problem behaviour, and settling into the new job.

Two years into the apprenticeship, it came to a grinding halt when he became unwell. He was eventually diagnosed with chronic fatigue. He was only able to pick up part-time work doing repairs in a hotel. He was home more, using pot three to four times a week and he became noticeably more depressed and harder to live with. I asked him to stop smoking marijuana. His response was, "It helps me cope. You don't understand how hard my life is, it's ok for you, you just go to work."

I was paying all the bills – food, mortgage, two car loans, his child maintenance payments, numerous flights for the other child's visits with us, as well as singing, swimming and cheerleading lessons for the other children. He only paid for his fuel, cigarettes and marijuana.

One child's bad behaviour worsened rapidly, becoming more violent, smashing walls, breaking furniture and stealing money from the house. Also due to poor behaviour at school, staff recommended that family services should be contacted. A few months' later family services moved the child into a foster home.

Then his other child came to live with us permanently, such a great kid. I enjoyed being involved and doing fun things with the children. However, I could see his depression creeping in again. I saw a counsellor and tried to find ways to improve his self-confidence. With the problem child no longer in the house we also decided it was the right time to have a child of our own, and we were soon blessed with a happy, healthy baby. His parenting style was casual and playful – not much focus on the discipline side, but fun when it came to playing with the kids.

My career was moving ahead and I was promoted to Area Manager of the northern part of the country. He quit the job doing repair work at the hotel to start his own business. It provided money for his expenses, which were actually increasing as he was smoking marijuana four to five times a week at home during the day. I hated this and addressed it with him. His response was, "You're just jealous that I've got so many friends. Stop hassling me. You are not liked as I am. You are too straight and no fun."

He spent most of his time at home so decided he would be a stay-at-home parent. He really enjoyed the role, despite it not sitting well with his ego. He did tell me though that if I wanted him to continue being the home parent, I would have to pay him. As he was not going out to work anyway I decided I might as well use the fact that he was at home and I agreed. Despite earning this money and the money from his part-time business, he contributed no money to the household. I did ask and his response was. "I'm taking care of the baby. You've got a good job and I never ask you to pay for my marijuana. I can't understand why you're complaining. I may not give the house any money but I save you money."

One year after my first child's birth, my boss offered me a

promotion to State Trainer, which meant a move back to the city. He had no employment commitments, so we figured the move would be better for the children with university not far off, if that was the way they wanted to go. We once again thought it would be a fresh start. We had a number of discussions about him getting back into work and contributing to the household, but even though he began a job as a maintenance manager, he never put any money into the family household budget. His response was always the same: "You need to lighten up and stop bringing me down."

It only took six months before his marijuana use caused problems in his new job. Next he started a job as a night filler at a supermarket, which also only lasted about six months. He then decided to restart his own business, but the business went broke as he spent more money on cigarettes and marijuana than he earned.

I watched on, unable to stop his almost-daily marijuana use and the accompanying moodiness. None of us ever knew what his mood would be like when we got home. Some days we would find that he had slept all day, other days we would witness depressive episodes, and at other times super hyper moods bordering on manic behaviour. He was not involved with the family in any way now. His main activities were visiting mates and smoking marijuana.

I paid all the family and household bills but refused to provide money for drugs. He found a job through a mate as a sorter in a recycle centre. We had many discussions about him cutting down on the marijuana but his response was, "It doesn't affect you, you shouldn't be so uptight and always making me feel bad. You're the reason I smoke marijuana so much anyway."

I knew our relationship was shaky but we wanted another child and so I had our second child. I was the one paying for everything, so it was my responsibility anyway and he never minded more children. I also thought that just perhaps another baby would help him become more responsible.

Unfortunately, more smoking and manic episodes ensued. Less involvement with anything we did as a family was now the norm. Thank heavens my stepchild was so wonderful, helping a lot, walking to collect my eldest child from school, bringing the washing in, and starting dinner some nights. This child was wonderful with the new baby and sort of started taking on the role of the other parent in the house, mostly while my partner slept or sat out the back "pulling cones" – in front of the children now.

His moods became quite aggressive. Finally I got him to see a doctor who diagnosed bipolar disorder brought on by marijuana use. He refused to take the prescribed medication and his manic episodes became more frequent. He constantly produced business ideas that needed finance loans, such as soapstone carvings, making mini grandfather clocks using clock faces from the $2 shop, a worm farm, becoming a travelling clown and even becoming a race caller.

He constantly did peculiar things. For instance, one night when his car had broken down while visiting a friend, to get home he used his mate's son's BMX bicycle to ride to the railway station. But as no helmet was available he used an ice cream container tied on to protect his head, with the insistent belief that if the police were to look, they would never be able to tell the difference.

Finally, everything came to a head late one night, when he was displaying very manic behaviour after smoking a lot of pot. He was very aggressive and insisted that the next morning we were going to the bank and we were going to redraw $10,000 off the mortgage so he could buy an old car to do up. He believed the deal would make a profit of $4,000 and he told me that I would not stop this venture.

I said, "I don't think it's a good idea and I'm not prepared to do it."

With that, strong hands grabbed my throat and I heard the words, "Either you agree or I will kill you now."

I was afraid, but I firmly told him to take his hands off my throat. I ran and got my eldest child and put this child in the car. He locked me out of the house but I managed to squeeze in the cat door and grabbed my 18-month-old baby.

My thirteen-year-old stepchild stood in between us and said, "Just let her leave." I had to promise that I would come back in the morning. When I did and asked my stepchild to join me, who did.

We stayed in a hotel that night. The next morning I went to a solicitor.

After our separation there were a number of other manic or aggressive episodes, but one that lasted a number of hours really stands out. My children and I came home one Saturday afternoon to find him in the house despite the fact that there were rulings in place to stop him from coming near the home. He said he had moved back into his house. He continued sitting out the back smoking marijuana, eating pizza and behaving manically, ranting and raving about all sorts of ideas, plans and schemes. My request for him to leave the home was met with more aggression and refusal. Finally, I had to call the police. After barricading himself in the carport, it took eight police officers to get him out and off the property.

Despite his false taunts, I have some amazing friends who stood by me and supported me. One couple, who had a young child of their own, took me and my three children into their home the next day. We stayed with them for over a month. Another dear friend gave evidence in court to help put a protection order in place, as he had described to her how he was going kill me and dispose of my body.

Thanks to childcare, my friends and some family, I was able to care for my children and keep my job.

Unfortunately, this was not the end. My stepchild returned to the city at the request of his mother. We also had to go through all the legalities and have all the papers signed to sell the house and divide the assets. I did all this through a solicitor.

He only laid his hands on me once, that time when he put his hands around my throat, but I was not waiting around for another time! I believe it gets worse. I had suffered verbal abuse for years, listening to a constant rant of unkind words that led me to feel I was not worthy of friends, I was not sympathetic, not caring, not loving, not fun, too hard on myself (because I never drank or did drugs), too rigid, too boring, too stuck up and never did enough to help. I know now that this is not the case; it was his way of hurting me and tearing me down, making me feel worthless.

Making it on my own

I was now a single mother. I had to make it happen if I wanted to give my children everything I felt they should have. He never paid child support but I never expected that he would. When we were married he had not contributed to the family budget, so why would I expect payments to start now? I knew I needed more income to be able to put the children through private schools, pay for activities they wanted to do and go on overseas holidays. I had to come up with a strategy.

Six months after the separation, I bought a small home and paid it off in four and a half years. I had read that if you owned your home you could borrow against it, and that is what I did, one house at a time. From the small proceeds I got from the sale of our larger home I paid off my credit card and got rid of the personal loan (for his car) that was in both names. This meant I had just my mortgage so I paid two-and-a-half times the repayments. I could manage this as the mortgage was small (like the house). Once it was paid off, while still working full time, I went on to purchase, renovate and sell seven investment properties, making money on them all, sometimes a little and sometimes a bit more.

My strategy was to buy in the lower end of the market, do a basic renovation that included paint, curtains and blinds, new floor coverings, sometimes partial or full kitchen and bathroom renovations, tidy the yard and if necessary, demolish old yard structures. I did most of the work myself. Occasionally I had to get workmen in to do some heavy building work that I couldn't do, or work that was illegal for me to do, like plumbing or electrical. The other strategy was to do it all in six weeks. This meant I avoided paying a heap of interest. By the time I renovated, sold it and the sale went through, I usually had borrowed the money for three months. I always borrowed the full price of the purchase, plus enough for the stamp duty and three months interest payments as well. I put the renovation costs on a credit card, which I paid in full once the house sold. I always budgeted prior to buying. I learned to estimate an average amount for each thing that needed to be done, e.g. to carpet a house cost about $1200, to paint a house inside was $500, Stamp Duty $5,000 and so on. This way I could estimate, with all costs included, if I was likely to make a profit. I was virtually selling in the same market that I bought in. If the figures didn't stack up then I offered less or didn't buy.

I did not do up these houses to amass a housing portfolio. It was for additional income as I always bought and sold. I never bought, renovated and kept; I was not working on a "wealth creation" concept. I have included details at the end of this chapter for the fourth property I renovated, which shows the purchase price, costs and budget I estimated. Then I show what the actual costs were for the same property. I purchased this house for $190,000. It cost $31,490 for renovations, stamp duty and other costs and I sold six weeks later for $265,000, making a profit of $43,510. This is the house I made the most money on, but for most of the other houses I renovated I made profits of $7,000 (my lowest profit), $13,500 and $19,000. You don't need to make heaps; even making $5,000–$10,000 can be enough to put your child through one year of private school or to go on an overseas family holiday. On straight wages alone, it can take quite a while to actually save $10,000, but this way I could make it in twelve weeks. If you saved $100 per week it would take 100 weeks, which is two years to save this amount of money.

Strategies to survive and thrive

I had been fortunate to learn from a number of people a few factors that I lived by even when I was in a relationship. This allowed me to get out, stay out and start again.

I call these factors the **7 Protection Keys** and you can remember it as **OWNHOME**, outlined on the next page.

In the 15 years since my separation we have been on six overseas and numerous interstate holidays. My two children have enjoyed many extra curricular activities and both have attended private schools. The three of us now live in a larger house. I may move to a smaller place once they move out, but I will be happy to move alone, confident I can make it on my own.

I love and always remember this mantra: "Truly rich people don't have the most of everything; they just make the most of everything they have."

7 Protection Keys

1. **O**wn savings: Have a bank account of your own. You might have a joint account, but also having your own bank account with even a couple of thousand saved can make all the difference to your safety and that of your children and give you the ability to move on if you need to do that.

2. **W**ork: The personal and financial support could make the difference to you being able to cope and never go back. If you don't have a job, get one. Anything will do to start with. You can always change jobs later.

3. **N**o major credit: Don't run up a credit card bill that you cannot pay off yourself within one year.

4. **H**em in loans: Don't have more than one personal loan. Chances are if things go wrong you will be the one paying it. The best situation is not to have any personal loans if you can, especially as the interest is high.

5. **O**verpay mortgage: If you need time when you get out, you will be ahead on your payments. If you never need it, no worries – it will mean you pay off your mortgage sooner anyway.

6. **M**ove Small: If you find you are on your own, buy a small place with a small mortgage and pay it off quickly. Try to get a place that you could pay off in five to seven years.

7. **E**nterprises: To make additional income, find a rundown property in the lower end of market. Do the budget to see if it stacks up. If so, renovate in six weeks and pay your tax. You only pay tax if you MAKE money.

© Broken to Brilliant

House renovation budget plans

PLANNED BUDGET for Investment 4	
Investment	Costs
Purchase Price Stamp Duty Searches/legal fees/adjustments Commission on sale Interest on loan	$190,000.00 $5,000.00 $1,300.00 $6,500.00 $2,200.00
Total purchase cost	$205,000.00
Improvements	Costs
Bathroom Paint Curtains/ Blinds Garage wall Carpets Tiles Fence panel Bobcat and skip Electrician Gardens/gravel Sundries	$9,000.00 $500.00 $200.00 $500.00 $1,000.00 $400.00 $300.00 $400.00 $300.00 $400.00 $1,000.00
Total Improvements	$14,000.00
Total purchase plus improvements	$219,000.00

ACTUAL COST for Investment 4 and PROFIT	
Purchase Price	$190,000.00
Stamp Duty	$5,275.00
Searches/legal fees	$1,417.00
Commission on sale	$7,783.00
Interest on loan	$2,135.00
Total costs	$16,610.00
Total purchase price inc cost	$206,610.00
Improvements	Costs
Bathroom	$8,800.00
Garage wall	$750.00
Laundry	$825.00
Paint	$170.00
Timber	$19.00
Paint brushes etc.	$77.00
Cleaning products	$200.00
Vanity	$31.00
Tiles	$247.00
Paint	$133.00
Curtains	$61.00
Carpets	$1,064.00
Sundries	$54.00
Rods and tracks	$25.00
Paint	$345.00
Knobs	$50.00
Skip	$210.00
Bobcat	$206.00
Locks	$52.00
Outdoor light	$10.00
Light fittings	$41.00
Electrician	$188.00
Gravel	$597.00
Plants	$26.00
Fence	$238.00

Concrete	$9.00
Hardware	$52.00
Mirror	$65.00
Paint	$51.00
Laundry tub	$123.00
Toilet seat/bathroom access	$29.00
Light fitting bathroom	$12.00
House wash	$120.00
Total Cost	$14,880.00
Total costs: improvements, stamp duty, interest, commission	$31,490.00
Total purchase price plus all costs	$221,490.00
Sale price 6 weeks later	$265,000.00
Profit	$43,510.00

CHAPTER TWO

THERE IS GREAT STRENGTH IN GENTLENESS

"Does your partner always make you feel safe?"

A BUBBLY, TRUSTING, INTELLIGENT 21 YEAR-OLD GIRL MET AND fell head-over-heels in love with a charming and very attentive 24 year-old guy. When she finally had the courage to leave the relationship at the age of 38, she was a sad, broken and terrified mother with children to protect.

Names and categories for the types of abuse she experienced would be emotional, physical, sexual, judicial, spiritual, financial and any other word that can drum up terror in someone. When she looked back, it was hard to recognise the smashed shell of the woman she was now compared to the young woman she had been. She couldn't even look in the mirror without feeling shame. She was sure no-one would ever believe what her life had become.

Then there would be the judgement. She already had no respect for herself. But the core reality was, it just wasn't safe to even try to leave at this time.

If she'd been given a dollar every time someone told her how "lucky" she was to have a caring partner, then she would have been rich beyond her dreams. But behind closed doors it was the complete opposite: her living nightmare.

In the beginning, their dreams for their futures were very similar: emigrating to Australia with professions that guaranteed them citizenship. Within three months he had swept her off her feet and asked her to marry him. They grew more in love over the next two years and married. A week after getting married, they flew to Australia.

He became more attentive every day, always phoning her to see how she was, asking who she was with and where she was going. In the end, you never saw them apart. Why, he'd even have his hand around the back of her neck all the time, like he was "steering" her. So attentive and very charming, it was so intense it became terrifying.

At other times, he would taunt her, frighten her, make her feel anxious about things outside the home... and inside it. The world began to scare her and he would tease her that she was "frightened of everything". She didn't like being teased but she loved him unconditionally so she would try as hard as she could to always please him, to keep him happy.

She felt controlled, isolated from all other support, dependant on him. He said he was the only one she was safe with, that he could protect her from everything and everyone. He would bad-mouth and ridicule everyone to her but continue to be charming to their faces. Slowly as the years rolled on, the terror escalated and she soon heard the serious threats of:

> *"If we separate, I'll get EVERYTHING! I'll get the house, the car, the money, the kids and I'll stand up in court and*

tell everyone you're mad and get you locked away."

To make sure she feared him, he would delight in looking over maps in front of her, pointing out disused mineshafts and explaining how a dead body could be dumped down a mineshaft and NEVER be found. Even if it were, he'd say:

"If you burn it, then they can't see the DNA to identify the body."

Due to his profession, this statement powerfully convinced her how easy it would be to get away with it. Please bear in mind that when you live in terror 24 hours a day, seven days a week, are isolated and sleep deprived, it is so convincingly believable.

So why did she stay?

For many reasons, she stayed, feeling petrified of possible retaliation. She had taken her wedding vows in the belief that with love and support they could overcome anything. She chose to become a mother to his children and always envisaged the children having their father there, like the clichéd "normal" family.

Because they kept moving around, she became more and more isolated from family and friends. There were 15 homes in 13 years of the relationship. Everyone thought they were the perfect couple with the perfect lifestyle. There was nowhere safe to run to with the kids in the country towns they lived in. Besides, who would believe her over him? He was so charming and caring; no-one would believe the things she would say, because they were the opposite of what he portrayed to the outside world especially now that he was a caring emergency services professional. To walk away would mean risking everything they had both worked so hard to achieve. They say the more you have to lose, the harder it is to leave. She could certainly relate to that.

It just was not safe for her to try to leave. There was no way she would risk her children's lives. Also, her faith in God kept her going. You are supposed to forgive and try everything you can to be a perfect loving wife. She remembered the vows she had taken on her wedding day, through the good times and bad times. He would always minimise the bad times – was she really over-exaggerating the terror she felt? He would taunt her constantly saying she was frightened of "everything."

Nobody truly knew what the terror was like behind closed doors. In conversations afterwards, he was so convincing, saying he HAD to treat her like that; she had AGAIN pushed his buttons. So again, it was HER fault. The injuries he generously gave her were always in places that could be hidden under her clothes. He never touched her face. Her doctor even had her blood tested for its ability to clot, as she had so many bruises. He would minimise his abuse by saying she had "peach skin" that bruised extra easily. The objects he smashed in anger were never his belongings, only hers. He could switch back to being the charmer when someone came to the door. He learned to taunt her when she tried to hide her tears and shaking hands as she tried to compose herself in front of the visitors.

Even when the first child was born, and he stayed in a swag on the floor by her side in the hospital, and insisted on doing the baby's first bath, the midwives said how "lucky" she was to have him. Little did anyone know that he would refuse to let her comfort or feed her distressed baby; it was the worst torture to terrify her. As the children got older, he found many cruel ways to withhold the children from her to get her to "behave" and do as she was told.

Many times she would be locked outside, hearing her children crying to be comforted and breastfed. She would have to hold it together, so that he would let her back in sooner than later. On one occasion with the first child, he physically restrained her from comforting and feeding the baby for nearly four hours using the "controlled crying technique" he had read about. It took all her negotiating skills to convince him to phone a family health helpline. They told him it was too long to let a four-month-old baby cry. But she had to be careful when she was finally able to hold the child, not to have him perceive it as a loss to him, otherwise that would put the child and her in more danger.

He decided when the second child would be weaned from her breastfeeding. He sent her off on long walks with an aching heart, fighting back tears while he tried to settle the child. He said she was making the child too dependent on her and this was detrimental to him developing a stronger bond with the child.

When one of the children, after three days of high fevers and fitting, finally developed the rash showing they had life-threatening meningococcal septicaemia, he said she was dramatising it all to embarrass him in front of his hospital colleagues! He said she obviously had Munchausen by Proxy Syndrome (MBPS).

He'd take the children camping out bush, but refuse to tell her where he was going or for how long. She would be left at home to return to work. Her stress levels were high. It was incredible that she was able to function at work. People would ask her, "So where are they exactly? When are they coming back?" She would hide behind a brave smile and say, "I'm not sure, but they'll be back soon." When they did return she'd have to hide her anxiety from him or this would irritate him and cause another fight. He would accuse HER of being the control freak and not trusting him as a father.

The cycle of violence was played over and over: the build-up phase, the explosion, then apologising and flying high on the honeymoon phase until the build-up happened again. He always bought beautiful bunches of flowers to say how sorry he was, and made the most AMAZING promises of how this would be the last time they would fight like that. She came to know them as "sorry flowers" and dreaded them. Again, visitors to the house would tell her how lucky she was to have such beautiful bouquets from her husband. If only they knew! His amazing promises included that this would be the last time they would fight like that. He would wipe the slate clean, another new beginning. He would ALWAYS have an excuse for his behaviour and he would always say it was HER fault that she MADE him act that way. She knew how to push his buttons, so if she could just be a good girl and behave, then he wouldn't have to treat her the way he did.

But nothing she ever did wrong could EVER justify him putting his hands around her throat to stop her breathing…or could it? No, he'd say:

"I wasn't choking you Babes; I was just squeezing your neck."
"I wasn't kicking you; I was moving you with my foot."
"I wasn't hurling you against the wall; I was restraining you."

The excuses went on and on until, with terror destroying her sense of reality, she just did not have the energy to argue anymore. When the family dog went for him when he was "restraining" her, she got the blame for even that:

"You've even turned the dog against me."

When she did try to explain herself to him he'd label her an "Argumentative Bitch", and when she kept her mouth closed and did as she was told, then he yelled at her she was a "Miserable Bitch", so there was no way she could do it right. When he was in one of THOSE moods, she had to be very careful to give him enough of a fight to feed his appetite for control but not too much to put her life in danger. It was all so exhausting!

We all know there are low "bad times" but there are also fantastic "good times". It's like a roller coaster ride until the thrill becomes constant terror. You are hanging on for dear life because he's now arced it up and removed the seatbelts and brakes. Then in an instant, he could be the gentlest, most romantic man in the world.

At the end, she was exhausted all the time, trying to keep up with his moods. The term some counsellors use is "battle weary" and God, it sums it up so well. She was petrified when he was physically there as well as when he wasn't. He constantly taunted her that she was mentally unstable, "An Effing Psycho Bitch, always overreacting to everything".

Even being in the car wasn't safe. He'd delight in making sudden jerks around corners, so her head would bang against the window, or slamming on the brakes for no reason – anything to terrify her. He would hide things in odd places and deny he'd touched them and say, "See Babes, you're going mad!" He'd secretly steal money out of her purse and deny it. On night duty he'd sneak home and leave the front door open, saying it was her fault and she had put the children at risk. It was when she caught him tipping out half her coffee and trying to say that she was mad because she couldn't remember drinking it, that she knew it had all gone too far.

Eventually they moved back to the city and she started counselling. Surprise, surprise: she wasn't mad or bad, just incredibly sad. She was immediately asked to make a safety plan as it was clear how dangerous the situation really was. A light went on in the dark tunnel. She no longer believed everyone when they told her how "LUCKY" she was to have this charming man in her life. The gentle, loving soulmate had all but disappeared. This monster, which had only shown its ugly head occasionally in the beginning, was now out of control. She could see the Monster was the REAL personality behind the façade.

The last time she was assaulted, it was the ONLY time she physically fought back. She knew if she didn't, the hands around her throat would not be removed until she was dead.

She had never left before because she was petrified of retaliation. She was correct in her fears. The police helped her put a violent restraining order (VRO) in place. She believed this also protected the children, who were in her care. He retaliated the next day by taking the children from their schools, telling the Government Department and the Court that SHE was the crazy one and was not fit to be a mother.

He insisted she be "supervised" when seeing her children for the longest five months of her life. He tried to humiliate her even further by insisting that her "Supervisors" be her two best friends, normal women who had absolutely no qualifications in supervising an allegedly-crazy woman seeing her children. He tried to barter with her saying, "If you cancel your violent restraining order on me, I'll let you see the kids unsupervised." Even then, he minimised the fear he had caused her by seeing the VROs as a tit-for-tat payback.

At the police's recommendation, she spent time in a refuge for physical protection. She experienced the legal system at a financial cost of over $70,000. He worked the system to every extreme to drag things out. He nearly succeeded in breaking what little spirit she had left, but he underestimated the strength of this mother's love to protect her children. With the amazing support and belief of her friends, family and Support Services she survived this period too.

Many months later, after the second clinical psychologist interviewed ALL members of the family, it was AGAIN found that she was not crazy, but she was a survivor of domestic terror and he was the perpetrator. She battled the legal system for her young children's voices to be heard. They knew right from wrong. They knew when they were safe and when they were not. She wanted THEM to decide if they wanted to go on access visits to him.

The children blossomed and received a fantastic education, and confidence from government psychologists. Due to the professional therapeutic relationships made over many months, they made several eloquent disclosures. The current system needs to be reviewed when these children's voices are not heard by the system that is set up to protect them. Instead, they were further abused by being asked to repeat the disclosure to support workers. They were expected to disclose frightening personal accounts to complete strangers, again. Of course, they were too frightened and embarrassed to do so. So no action was taken. In his eyes, he was now able to "restrain" his children with no mother there to interfere this time.

She was then damned by the Support Agency he involved, saying she was "withholding" the children. Yet another support service told the mother that if she let the children go on unsupervised visits then she was not acting as a protective and safe mother! Once again, she felt trapped between a rock and a hard place. It was very similar to her attempts to leave in a safe way. So had anything changed since leaving? **Now she wasn't there to keep her children safe when in the father's care.**

Finally, after many years following the current court system, the children were placed in the mother's care 100%. The relationship was like a slowly sinking boat, only kept afloat by her furious bailing out of the water leaking in. She had to keep her head down and focused. She was kept frantic trying to keep the boat from sinking. He sat opposite her, hurling threats of abuse, lashing out with words and hands. Terrifying! She sat her children behind her so she could protect them with her body. He threatened her: "If you try to leave, I'll get everything, the house, the money, the car, the kids and I'll tell everyone you're mad. Anyway, you'll never survive because there are sharks in the water, and they'll get you AND the kids if you even THINK about taking them!" At least if she stays she can protect the kids. When she occasionally sneaks a look up, she panics, because she can't even see which direction the land is in, there isn't ANY land on any horizon to swim to! It's not safe to even TRY to leave.

Would YOU risk jumping into the water leaving your children behind?

That was MY story. On that last day of abuse, with my last bit of energy, I grabbed the children, jumped into the water and swam like hell to the shore. His boat didn't sink. It drifted a bit out to sea but I can always hear his voice. But as my education and confidence grows, so does my desert island of safety and sense of self.

How health professionals can screen for domestic violence

I am a survivor of domestic violence or domestic TERROR as I prefer to call it, and I am a health professional. So how do health professionals ask the question? There is definitely a desperate need for universal screening, the same as we routinely screen for pressure injuries, falls or alcohol abuse. However, I feel we need to look at emotional abuse as the first indicator, not physical abuse. There is ALWAYS emotional abuse at the start, only sometimes does it escalate to physical abuse and then more rarely to murder.

No-one was EVER brave enough to ask me if I felt SAFE around my partner. Health professionals only passed judgement on how "LUCKY" I was, to have such a charming partner who was so involved in everything I did. If I had been asked, sure, I might have initially been too scared to answer truthfully. However, each time I was then asked, the seed of confidence would have sprouted, until eventually, I know I would have had the courage to reply, "Actually, no, I do not always feel safe around my partner."

Realistically, it is only if you have walked this path that you may automatically pick up on it, without universal screening. The silence needs to be broken. The questions need to be asked. The domestic terror survivors need to be involved in developing a validated screening tool. The most important question in my view should be as simple as:

"Does your partner always make you feel safe?"

This is just as important to ask for same sex couples as heterosexual couples. Unfortunately, the statistics are the same for all intimate relationships.

Health professionals and government and social systems need to help break the silence that is suffocating victims. Child protection is everyone's business. This includes keeping mothers safe to be able to protect their children. By blaming mothers you are encouraging the perpetrators, allowing them once again to not be accountable for their actions. The mothers are NOT responsible for the father's behaviours. When you judge and condemn mothers, you make mums retreat even more. You reinforce the idea that silence is best. You are helping to put the children's safety further at risk, which no-one intentionally wants to do. Their self-esteem is already being battered regularly by the perpetrators. They do not need further abuse from health professionals and the system.

We, as health professionals, are also human. We need to educate ourselves, nurture ourselves, so that we do not feel confronted by asking the questions. We then need to realise that we are purely screening, identifying and then referring. I like to refer to this as the 3 R's: Recognising, Referring then Reflecting.

Recognise – Recognise domestic terror by asking one simple question: "Does your partner always make you feel safe?" Do you always feel safe around your partner?

Referral – Make a competent referral to appropriate services and/or health professional e.g. hospital, police, the national counselling helpline, information and support 1800 737 732, community services organisations like Centrecare.

Reflect – Reflect for your self-care needs, hold a debrief session with a team member/leader or work support service so that you can keep doing the amazing work you are already doing.

That is all. I am not saying that it will not take huge confidence and courage to ask the question, but it takes far more courage to survive the abuse and answer the questions truthfully.

We are simply offering choices. We are not responsible if people don't take up the offer. We are only consistently offering a choice, for when the victims are ready or feel safe to make a different choice. I never chose to be a Survivor, but every time I share my story publicly, I always get at least two brave women approach me afterwards to say they could also relate to my story. People that are more famous are choosing to share their stories in the media to also break the silence and educate us all.

Ask any Survivor what still bothers them years after leaving the relationship. What wakes them up with nightmares? What form of abuse remains, despite all the counselling? You can learn to turn the volume down on it, but the voice can still be clearly heard. It's the EMOTIONAL abuse. There is ALWAYS emotional abuse at the start, it may escalate to physical abuse and it's most extreme form, murder. That is why the term "domestic terror" better encompasses all the HORROR of this abuse. Even to some men that do the hurting, the perpetrators, it is a "terror": their behaviour even frightens themselves.

The more control and power a perpetrator gets, the more ferocious their appetite becomes. Their appetite is insatiable. However, as a victim, you learn that to survive you have to try to give more. The only crime you are guilty of is giving unconditional love. In a healthy relationship, the only thing we all strive to give and receive is unconditional love. **Let me repeat that: the ONLY thing Survivors are guilty of is giving unconditional love.**

My burning passion with domestic terror is to try to gently educate so that more people understand what it is. Hopefully, if you find yourself in that situation you can recognise it so that you can leave safely. If you can understand it you hopefully won't carry it out or perpetrate it, so that you too can have a healthy relationship, both giving and receiving unconditional love. That way your life can be enriched by the relationship. Everyone's a winner, everyone's happy, everyone's SAFE.

I don't believe any little boy wants to grow up with the ability to terrorise their loved ones. It doesn't make the perpetrators happy, but they need education and support to also be able to love unconditionally.

In Australia, one in three women will experience an abusive relationship at some stage in their lives and one in two women if you identify as Aboriginal. Isn't it time as a community that we do something about it? It's often called the silent crime, because of the view that what happens behind closed doors should stay there. This only empowers the perpetrators even more. Many women are too scared to speak out for fear of being judged a "bad" mother, and fear of having their children removed from their care by authorities. The biggest power behind silence about abuse is often the threats of what the perpetrator says he will do if the mother speaks out. Education and support need to surround the mother and children, and a safety plan is put in place so they can safely leave the relationship.

I see regular media stories of murder or maiming where a woman has tried to leave an abusive relationship but has not managed to do it safely. Research backs this up. The most dangerous time for a Survivor is when she is trying to leave. I myself can attest to this.

People will often ask, "Why did your relationship end?" My reply is always, "It wasn't safe to stay anymore." As the conversation develops, people will often ask, "Why didn't you just leave?" or "You wouldn't catch me putting up with that!"

The reality is that domestic terror is a complex, slow, insidious disease that you can only identify the beginning of once you've escaped. It's not like an abuser walks up to you and hurts you straight away. They do everything they can to charm you, to make you fall in love and they do EVERYTHING they can to get to know ALL about you, so they can then use that information to terrorise you.

I am an intelligent woman and now a thriving survivor. Abuse can happen to anyone, anywhere, from any background. Please don't judge us who have tried to love unconditionally. Nurture and support us to redirect our unconditional love to heal our children and ourselves, and to improve our community. Let us be heard. Ask US how to improve our communities. We have SO much to give, if only you will let us.

— A friend's perspective —

When my friend first told me about what had been going on I was shocked. I couldn't understand how I didn't know what was happening. I knew she was stressed with young children and working full time. The family had moved so often, she had lived in so many places – 15 homes in 13 years.

I had no idea how to help her deal with the situation. All I could do was be there for her and not judge her.

The one thing I could do was help her to see her children. During the time she was not able to be alone with her children, I was an 'approved' supervisor. I had to collect them from their father and take them to meet their mother in a park or similar, for her to spend time with them. I used to feel sick at the thought of having to do this, but if I didn't do it, she wouldn't get to see her children.

It was heart-wrenching having to take them away again at the end of the visit. Getting them into my car, most times in tears, with their mum trying to be strong and not cry. Taking them back to their father was one of the hardest things I have had to deal with emotionally.

I am in awe of how she has turned her life around and become a wonderful mother, has been recognised in her field of work and is actively involved in increasing awareness of domestic violence and trying to make changes.

Checklist for health professionals

- A first indicator – look for emotional abuse.
- Educate yourself about domestic violence.
- Nurture yourself.

3 R's: Recognising, Referring then Reflecting

1. **Recognise** – Recognise domestic terror by asking one simple question: "Does your partner always make you feel safe?"

2. **Referral** – Make a competent referral to appropriate services and/or health professional e.g. hospital, the police, the National Counselling Helpline, information and support 1800 737 732, community services organisations like Centrecare Support service, to set up a safety plan so they can safely leave the relationship.

3. **Reflect** – Reflect for your self-care needs, hold a debrief session with a team member/leader or work support service so that you can keep doing the amazing work you are already doing.

© Broken to Brilliant

CHAPTER THREE

PIECES TO A BETTER LIFE

"Contribution is an incredibly uplifting and empowering act of kindness. It lifts your soul, ignites passion and motivates you to do more for others. It heals in a way that nothing else can."

As I stood staring at the window, curtains draped behind me and one hand grasping the latch, my chest rose with every breath as I tried to calm my pounding heart. Who would have thought that my biggest and hardest achievement would be to simply close a window? One year on and the torment still played out in my head as the fear consumed me. Sure, there were many cold nights that I should have closed the window, but I could never bring myself to close it all the way. Just a one-inch gap was all that was needed to set my mind at ease.

Leaving it open meant giving in to fear and showed that the past still had power over me, but closing it meant I had to face that fear. I stood there for what seemed like hours, hearing my inner voice demand I take control, and that I was stronger and more powerful than all I had been through. I was trapped in thoughts that were not my own. They were forced there from the past.

But I did know the difference, I had experienced better and I knew what was right. It was in recognising my truth that I knew I needed to close the window.

Tears rolled down my face and my hand shook. Ten years on and I still find this hard to talk about and it tears me up. I laugh at myself and think how silly this must sound to others. But the truth is, when you live in fear, you live in a mindset of safety plans where you think, "How do I get out of here alive?", always thinking about how to keep the peace and how to calm his inner rage; making sure the windows are open so someone, somewhere, just might hear your screams for help…

As the latch on the window finally connected, I connected with myself. I knew at that moment if I was to move forward and have the life of my dreams, I had to create it. An overwhelming feeling of empowerment came over me from just closing the window. Imagine then how great the rest of my life was going to feel if I started facing my fears.

I started making plans and working on myself. At first I was not conscious of how I was going to do it or when, but I knew I was doing it.

Years before the final chapter of our relationship was over, I had a very vivid dream. Someone sat beside me on my bed with a book and as they turned the pages I could see what I was going to do with my life. It was all laid out before me. The next morning I woke with enthusiasm and excitement. I knew what I was going to do with my life! I was going to teach manners and beauty. This dream was not going to be taken from me! It was the one dream that would give me the strength to carry on through to the end of the relationship and give me the focus to begin a new life.

At that time, I had no idea that my vision and dream job would also be my greatest teacher. It saved me emotionally and physically. As my work continued, so did my passion and enthusiasm to learn and to become a shining example of what I believed a lady should be. The more I learned, the more respect for myself and others I gained. As I grasped how important morals and values were to me, the stronger my values became.

I fell in love with the meaning of etiquette: "to build relationships rather than tear them apart", to show respect, honesty and consideration, not just towards others but also towards myself. Contribution is also an incredibly uplifting and empowering act of kindness. I discovered it lifts my soul and ignites my passion and motivates me to do more for others. It heals me in a way that nothing else can.

I found my purpose in life was teaching manners and beauty to those who need it the most, like abused children; or to inspire ladies to fulfil their dream. It let me see that I was not alone in my struggles and there were so many people worse off than I ever was.

I found confidence from manners, as they are the do's and don'ts that show us what to expect in different situations. Believe me, when you have been kept away from the world or have had limited life experiences, learning what to expect and how to handle yourself in different situations really does boost your confidence.

I will never forget when my beautiful new partner took me

away for the first time and asked me to call room service; I almost died on the spot from the stress. Having to do anything new and step out of my comfort zone is incredibly scary, even if it is simply to make a phone call. Thankfully, I was eager to learn. Whenever I did something new, it would set my heart racing. I would tell myself, "See, it's not so bad. I still have all my body parts. I survived." This really helped change my mindset when it came to taking on new things.

Looking after my health and appearance made me feel good and it built my self-esteem. Appreciating how I looked and putting effort into me made me feel special. I also learned the value in this when teaching others how to present themselves. Teaching makeup techniques, haircare and how to style themselves could change a person's perspective. Capturing this in a photo gave them something to remind them of their true beauty.

I did not stop there. I went further. I studied, read and indulged in anything that improved my mind and how I looked at life. I immersed myself in courses that transformed how I felt about my past and myself. I took time out to rest if I needed it and slept a lot as well – funny how your body needs time to recover. I started to look at life as a lesson instead of a challenge. I got excited whenever I had light bulb moments, when things finally sunk in. No sooner did I learn that lesson than another would be right around the corner waiting for me.

I remember feeling like it was never going to end. Constant obstacles would bring me to breaking point. I also learned that it is okay to just break down and cry and feel like giving up – it was the Universe telling me to sit in the moment and just feel. It was in these moments I would normally find the answer and my strength to keep going. I jokingly would tell myself, "You're on the catch-up program and there are a lot of life lessons to learn. So they just laid them on you thick and fast!"

I also realised I was not Superwoman, but I was strong enough to deal with whatever lessons life threw my way. I truly believe we are here to learn the meaning of life. The only way to do this is to discover it in all its forms and learn how to deal with different situations. The better we deal with them, the faster we get through them. So I focused on learning better ways of dealing with negative situations, but this took me time and lots of trial and error.

Nothing happened overnight. In fact it took years of searching for answers in all the wrong places. For eight long years, I divulged my life story to every pair of ears that was unfortunate enough to be within listening distance. The verbal diarrhoea flowed from my mouth whether I knew the person or not. I grew aware of this, yet I had no filter, control, or way of stopping myself. I would repeatedly tell myself, "Whatever you do, do not talk about your stuff this time!" – and without fail I would! My poor family and friends – mainly my mother and partner – would have to endure this every time they spoke to me. I am sure they dreaded my calls. Surprisingly, they are both still in my life.

My inability to filter what I talked about was destroying my chances to build healthy relationships with others. So I decided to find out why I was continuing to do this and took a deeper look inwards. I discovered that I was so desperate to fix my past and my present situation that I was in search of the answer, a magic pill and a quick fix that would put an end to all my problems.

I soon learned that no-one had the answer. Nothing anyone said resonated with me. So I continued to talk and talk and talk some more, in search of the answer. The torture continued in one way or another to play out in my life. All this talking kept the past in control of my life.

Now I must confess, I was a slow learner. Sometimes I just had to experience things over and over before I had any light bulb moments. I probably read it somewhere or someone may have even told me, but I just didn't get it and therefore it wouldn't register with me. I had to experience it for myself. This taught me a valuable lesson that has rung true for me and stayed with me.

So after eight years of searching, I finally had the "aha" moment. I realised that the more you talk about things, the more you keep them present in your life. The universe hears you and thinks you're asking for more. Sure enough, it delivers more of the same.

Only talk about the things you want in your life. My grandson is the perfect example of this, as are most children. If I say the words "don't do" at the start of the sentence, then he will do what I just asked him not to do. The universe, your body and children, miss hearing the word DON'T.

The wonderful saying, "speak of the devil and he will appear", couldn't be any truer. I can pretty much guarantee if I mentioned my past, then it would appear in some form. So, I learnt the hard way, all that talking I was doing, was keeping the past in control and dictating my life. I had to learn to shut up.

The answer finally resonated with me enough that I took action. I had studied Neuro Linguistic Programming (NLP) and used a tool from this to assist in closing my mouth. I would place my index finger over my lips with my chin resting in my thumb and my other fingers curling inward. This looks like you're thinking, so no-one will notice. Once I realised the power in this and that it was working – the past was now out of my life – I finally experienced some peace in my life. I am also very aware that even if someone else brings up domestic violence or my past, I keep it brief and leave the past out of it.

Counselling, for me, was a waste of time. It created a space for me to vent and bitch and talk about the past, which continued to keep the past in my life. Through all the reading, study, life lessons and personal growth, I was able to tell the counsellor why I would react or behave in certain ways. This led to them asking me why I was there.

I also noticed that when the past does raise its ugly head, at home we would fall back into old behaviour patterns. But now we can snap ourselves out of it by recognising what we are doing and drawing it to the attention of each other. It is constant work to change and improve, but it doesn't have to be hard. Learning to enjoy the journey is part of the process.

The choices we made in life that got us to where we are today all come from ourselves. Not our parents, not our partners. They came from us.

Yes, at some point, I chose this life. Sure, I fought this concept and said many times, "Like hell I chose this path. These people have no idea what they are talking about." But they were right.

I had heard and read many times that we make these choices,

and that what we hear as a child can affect us as adults. I sat with this for a while and while reading one night it hit me. I remembered a time when I was about four years old, listening to a story at Sunday school. We were told that there are two paths in life. One was straight, smooth and full of riches, gold and jewels. The other was a rough, rugged goat track that twisted all over the place. The teacher asked us which path we would take. Everyone said the smooth path as it sounded so lovely, and with that they snapped at us. They leaned towards us and with a stern look told us that we would all go to hell. They struck the fear of hell into us. Every child in that room sat in shock, staring straight back at the teacher in silence with jaws dropped.

I remember telling myself that I was going to take the roughest, toughest path I could find, as I was determined I was going to heaven. So at four years old I chose to take the hard way, and – surprise, surprise – I did. Now once I realised this I jumped on the phone and called my mother, like you do, and told her. Sure, my family think I am a little weird at the best of times but I am not changing for anyone, and I am sure they wouldn't want me to either.

Now as an adult I could see that I was still on this path. It was my four-year-old self that was keeping me there. I was young, vulnerable, gullible and naïve and I believed every word. However, as an adult I knew better and decided to get off that goat track. I started enjoying a smoother path.

That was around the time I discovered not to talk about what I didn't want in my life anymore. I must say, my life got a whole lot easier from that point on. Don't get me wrong, I am still learning, still growing and still getting through different blocks in my life. Sometimes, just out of the blue, something new will pop up that I felt I had already dealt with, or didn't know was a problem. I just look at it differently now and question if my belief comes from the mindset of me as a child or am I dealing with it as the adult me.

Practice makes perfect... I cannot tell you enough that your thoughts and words really affect your life, so choose them wisely. Just about all self-help books tell you the same thing. Why? Because it is true! You need to break the cycle for yourself and your children. Become aware of limiting words, thoughts and behaviours that you and others instal in yourself and your children. Become their role model and lead by example.

Challenge yourself to do better. Shake yourself off whenever you fall. Never punish yourself for not succeeding the first time. Practice makes perfect, and like me, you may need more attempts than others. Laugh at things and never take things too seriously – it's part of your journey.

Improve... You must, without a doubt, improve yourself. Grow, learn and work on yourself as much and as often as you need to. Spoil yourself at every chance you can. If you are feeling run down and falling apart, then you are no good to anyone, especially if you have children. This will keep you a vulnerable victim who will more likely make bad choices when your self-esteem is low. Take a step every day towards your goals and your dreams, even if it's just one. Reward yourself with every step. Change the way you look at life and start enjoying it. Do something every day that makes you feel good, even if it's just singing along with the radio. Take more pride in your appearance and your clothes, and develop routines or rituals that end up becoming habits. I just can't leave the house without my skincare routine done, or my skin feels yuck. I take great pride in looking after my skin. Take better care of your health and make better lifestyle choices. Nurture and love yourself because you're worth it. When you find beauty in everything, including yourself, then you have replaced hate with gratitude.

Empower... Find strength in yourself and do things that make you stretch and grow as a person. Acknowledge every time you complete or achieve something and allow yourself to be proud. Take that energy to motivate you to do something else. Climb a mountain – I did and I am still on top of the world because of this and now I know I can do anything. Stay in the truth and take control of your actions and reactions. Discover the power of forgiveness and see that people are doing the best they can with what they have. Empathy is a beautiful quality. When you realise why people do what they do, you become more settled. Rid yourself of negative people and old behaviour patterns that no longer serve you. Stand up for yourself and be heard. Always come from a place of truth, especially when it comes to your children, and it's important if you're going through a court hearing. The truth will always come out in the end and if you're not being honest with others, then you're only lying to yourself. Remember to stop thinking and reacting from the mindset of your child self and look at things from the adult you. Find your self-worth and remember you're stronger than you realise.

Checklist: If you are still in the same place or fighting with the past, a partner, family, friends or yourself, then you need to stop and review what you need to do to change this. Only YOU can change your life. Start with looking at your thoughts, your words and your actions. If you still feel resentment, anger, bitterness, regret, hate or blame, then you need to work on yourself. Find out what you need to do to move past this negative block.

Enlighten… Look at things through the eyes of love, consideration and acceptance. Learn that everyone is dealing with life the best way they know how, with the tools they have been given, even if they are not the correct tools. Keep a gratitude journal and write everything down that you are grateful for at the end of each day. Find beauty in everything and take time out to enjoy the simple things like relaxing in nature. Meditate, allow your soul to heal and learn to quieten your mind. One of the best things I ever did, and I highly recommend it, was Reconnective Healing. This gave me greater peace than anything else I ever tried. Look up social groups or classes that help you find peace and balance in your life, like walking groups or yoga classes. Get involved in volunteering in the community and give back – this feels wonderful and is so rewarding. Someone told me to ask Archangel Michael to watch over me and to protect me, so now whenever I feel nervous or scared I call upon him. He has not let me down once, I even ask him to watch over my children. Breathe, sleep, relax and enjoy life for a change, you're worth it.

When you see the value of the lessons you have gained, then you will have replaced resentment with empathy. When you fill your heart with love then you have replaced hurt with compassion.

Start now ... to put the PIECES of your life back together

If you're still talking about your past then you're not living in the present moment and nothing will change. You can't do the same thing and expect a different outcome. It is up to you, it is your choice. What will you choose?

P	**Practice makes perfect** • Your thoughts and words really affect your life, so choose them wisely. Become aware of limiting words, thoughts and behaviours that you and others instal in yourself. • Challenge yourself to do better. • Practice makes perfect, you may need more attempts than others. • Laugh at things and never take things too seriously – it's part of your journey.
I	**Improve...** • Improve yourself. Grow, learn and work on yourself as much and as often as you need to. • Spoil yourself at every chance you can – if you are feeling run down and falling apart, then you are no good to anyone. • Take steps every day towards your goals and your dreams – even just one. • Reward yourself with every step. • Change the way you look at life and start enjoying it. • Do something every day that makes you feel good, even if it's just singing along with the radio. • Take more pride in your appearance, your clothes, and develop routines or rituals that end up becoming habits. • Nurture and love yourself because you're worth it. • Find beauty in everything, including yourself. • Replace hate with gratitude.

© Broken to Brilliant

Start now ... to put the PIECES of your life back together

E	**Empower** • Find strength in yourself. • Do things that make you stretch and grow as a person. • Acknowledge your achievements. Be proud. • Stay in the truth and take control of your actions and reactions. • Discover the power of forgiveness. • Rid yourself of negative people and old behaviour patterns that no longer serve you. • Stand up for yourself and be heard. • Remember to stop thinking and reacting from the mindset of your child self and look at things from the adult you. • Find your self-worth and remember you're stronger than you realise.
C	**Create a checklist** • If you are still in the same place or fighting with others or yourself, stop and review what you need to do to change this. • Only YOU can change your life. • Start with looking at your thoughts, your words and your actions. • If you still feel resentment, anger, bitterness, regret, hate or blame, then you need to work on yourself. • If you're still talking about your past then you're not living in the present moment and nothing will change. • You can't do the same thing and expect a different outcome. It is up to you, it is your choice. What will you choose?

© Broken to Brilliant

Start now ... to put the PIECES of your life back together

E	**Enlighten** • Look at things through the eyes of love, consideration and acceptance. • Learn that everyone is dealing with life the best way they know how, with the tools they have been given, even if they are not the correct tools. • Keep a gratitude journal and write everything down that you are grateful for at the end of each day. • Find beauty in everything and take time out to enjoy the simple things like relaxing in nature. • Meditate, allow your soul to heal and learn to quieten your mind. • Get involved in volunteering in the community and give back. • Breathe, sleep, relax and enjoy life for a change, you're worth it. • See the value of the lessons you have gained. • Replace resentment with empathy. • Fill your heart with love.
S	**Start now** • Decide to change. • Face your fears. • Make a plan and take action. • Educate yourself and learn as much as you can – study, read and indulge in anything that will improve your mind and how you look at life. • Stop the verbal diarrhoea – the more you talk about things, the more you keep them present in your life. Only talk about the things you want in your life. • Enjoy the journey of change. • This was your choice – The choices made in life got you to where you are today, those choices all come from ourselves. Not our parents, not our partners. They came from us. Yes, at some point, you chose your life. Come to terms with this. • Choose your thoughts and words wisely.

© Broken to Brilliant

CHAPTER FOUR

BEGINNING WITH ME

"Make peace with yourself; know your own mind and heart."

I WAS RAPED.

I was 14, it was my first time and I was paralytic drunk.

My story is not particularly original or shockingly brutal, but what happened devastated me none the less. I had been invited to a sleep over at the local caravan park with a bunch of girls from my school. My closest friend was around my age but the other girls were all seniors and a few years older. We'd somehow convinced the parentals that it would be just us girls. This of course was code for "all night party". At the time, I was more concerned about getting the alcohol and looking cool rather than safety first. I was a naive kid trying to show off to my peers. It was cool to drink and you were even cooler if you could drink a lot. Yes, totally stupid and cliché.

The evening started off as any party does. We settled into our caravan and put away our bags, de-boxed the silver "goon" bags* and poured the highly classy $10.95 cask wine into the assorted chipped and well-used glasses provided by the establishment. It was exciting, breaking the rules and acting cool. All I can say

---

* Wine packaged in a silver bag inside a box.

now, when I look back is, "Really?" I mean, what the hell was I thinking?

We talked about what most girls talk about at that age. We bitched about teachers and how we hated school, swapped fashion tips and talked boys. Soon, however, we were joined by the senior guys. Showing off to each other, we played drinking games with cards and made stupid dares, nothing really too serious.

Finally, when I was almost to the point of throwing up, I somehow managed to get up on the top bunk at the back of the van with a doona and passed out.

I don't know how much time elapsed but I was woken with the full weight of another body pushing me into the mattress and a pair of rough lips covering my entire mouth. A great big tongue shoved down my throat suffocated me while unfamiliar hands groped all over my body. At first, I just went along with it. I was completely disoriented. Dead drunk is probably a better term.

At some stage I realised who the senior boy was. I was overwhelmed by the sexual attention but at the same time scared and a little embarrassed as to why I had woken up with him on top of me. I'm pretty sure I was unconscious when he started kissing me. I didn't even really know this guy let alone like him. I certainly wasn't sexually attracted to him nor was I ready for sex, but I didn't say anything.

The heavy petting started to get a bit too serious for me. All I wanted to do was go to sleep or throw up. I was still so drunk.

I have no idea why I thought this would be a good idea, but I asked him if he had a condom. I was thinking that this would deter him from continuing. Everyone knows that you can't have sex without a condom right? It wasn't safe and everyone knew that. I was just that naive. Somehow, in my head I had thought that this was the best alternative to saying no to him. I could avoid any unpleasant confrontation without the admission that I didn't want to have sex with him, because that wouldn't be cool. Offending people or causing confrontation is not in my nature and even as this was happening I didn't want to be impolite! I didn't want to be rude.

I was also a romantic idealist at that age and believed in the "one". I wanted the prince and the white horse. Well, I knew that I wanted my first time to be special and worth some kind of effort. I wanted my first time to be with someone that I loved and who loved me back.

I remember thinking how clever I thought I was. I had asked him if he had a condom knowing that he wouldn't have one. I had meant it as a no, not as my consent.

At first, he stopped and said he didn't have one just as I had suspected. I was relieved and advised that I didn't want to continue. He got down off the bunk and again I passed out into a drunken blackout. The next thing I remember is being pulled off the top bunk by my hair. I had no idea what was going on. I struggled a little but realised that the senior boy had returned. He pushed me down the small hallway of the van and out the door. I tried grabbing onto the bunks and digging in my heels but those hands on my back kept pushing me out the door. I even said, "Stop! I just want to go to sleep. Leave me alone!" But those hands kept pushing me into the cold night.

I re-emerged from unconsciousness with him pushing himself roughly into my body. I think I had blacked out. I was crying and saying "no" repeatedly but he kept saying "move faster". I was half-naked in the woods with him sticking his penis into me. I kept trying to get away, get him off but I was sluggish and lacking strength. I was totally shocked at what was going on.

I awoke again, later, to the cold of the night and the hard ground, with my pants and shoes strewn around me and my shirt half off. I must have passed out yet again. He had left me there, wherever "there" was – somewhere out in the woods.

I slowly rearranged myself as best I could and began to wander through the dry leaves and forest debris. I remember the crunching sound being so loud under my feet. As I struggled to sober up I was realising what had happened. Aimlessly walking through the trees I heard some voices and I followed them until I could see some lights. The caravan park was up ahead.

The senior boy who had raped me and left me in the woods had gone, but his two friends were still playing card games in the van. They were making fun of me, sickening grins from ear to ear asking, "How was it?" By this stage I was bleeding through my pants. I remember the embarrassment and humiliation I felt as I stood in the van hallway, ugly crying, blood running through my pants and down my legs while they both just sat at the end of the van staring at me, laughing.

I then woke up in the caravan park shower block. I was shocked into consciousness due to the cold water kicking in from the shower above. I had lost more time. These showers were apparently coin operated and the meter had run out. I was naked, balled up on the concrete floor, shivering uncontrollably and then everything hit me at once.

My mind was running through everything so quickly and I couldn't accept the circumstances I was in. But it was my feelings that were too hard for me to process. I can't even begin to explain how my emotions were affecting me. I couldn't seem to move from that spot. Actually, I physically didn't want to move from that spot, even though the water was freezing and all I wanted to do was go home to sleep where I felt safe.

I heard footsteps scuffing the concrete floor and I shrank back hoping I wouldn't be noticed. I then heard the distinct sound of coins dropping into a machine and the water gradually getting warmer. When I looked up through my wet hair, I saw a fourth senior boy leaning against the wall looking away from me with an expression of pity on his face. It took me some time to realise that he was helping me and that he had put coins into the meter for me.

"Thank you," I managed to emit in probably the smallest sounding voice ever to have escaped from my voice box. We stayed in this bubble for what seemed like eternity. He never spoke; he just stayed with me, leaning on the opposite wall at a distance. Every so often, he would leave for a bit and then come back with more coins for the shower.

I think we must have stayed like that for about three hours. When I was finally ready to leave the comfort of the water, I remember being completely pruney all over. Spots were dancing all over my eyes and my skin was really white.

The boy got me a towel, dried me and even dressed me. I

couldn't speak but I think he knew I wasn't really capable of doing anything at that point. It was surreal. After what had just happened, I didn't feel threatened or overly self-conscious with him present. Actually, I don't think I felt anything. I rarely look back to this memory but I know if it weren't for him, if he had not helped me, I may not have recovered.

Later, when I was dry and warm, he took me outside to the camping tables where I recognised one other person from our party. She was sitting on the table talking to another camper. When I sat down the camper started to talk to me. I can't remember what we were talking about initially, but he put his arms around me and started to lead me away from the table.

I was weak, devastated and emotionally drained and all I wanted was to curl up somewhere. This guy must have seen me as a target. The difference this time was that I was relatively coherent. Although I was still groggy from the alcohol, I was starting to sober up quickly.

He started feeling up my breast and kept leading me away from the group. When I realised that he was trying to lead me away for sex I tried to push him off, all niceties discarded. His grip on me tightened. He tried to really pull me towards his camping area when he realised I was trying to stop. I had to push him pretty hard the second time to get him to let go and then I actually verbally told him to leave me alone.

"Whatever, you fucking tease," he threw back at me as he wandered off to whatever snake pit he came from. I shrivelled up inside. So this was the real world.

I vaguely remember walking home after that. I left all my

stuff back in the van and just walked. I meandered in the dark, along the roadside, at about 4am in the morning and it took me two hours to get back home. All the while, I tried to remember what had happened but most importantly, I asked myself over and over again why it had happened.

After that, it seemed everyone at school knew. What happened to me was everywhere. Rumours of me being a slut whispered down most corridors. People talked behind my back or made fun of me wherever the chance arose. I played it like I didn't know what they were talking about and tried to make it look like it didn't affect me. I didn't want any more confrontation. I didn't want people looking or talking about me. I tried not to give them a reaction so they would leave me alone.

The boy who had raped me later approached me to see if I wanted to go again. He explained that he thought I was a good ride and that we should hook up again some other time. It was like he thought what had happened was totally ok. I suspect it was because I made that stupid decision to ask for a condom. I was in complete disbelief. What I felt at that time was the strongest sense of humiliation and disgust. A lot of this I felt for him, but actually more so towards myself.

The fact is I don't remember much of it because I had blacked out due to alcohol. I got drunk and lost control of myself. I'm pretty sure he knew I was paralytic that night but he did it anyway. I'm also certain he was in full control of all his faculties. I feel the people around me at that time didn't see it as rape because I was drunk. I was just another drunk chick who deserved what she got. I also blame myself because some small part of me believed that they were right – drunk girls are easy targets. Guys are studs and girls are sluts. That was how people thought back then.

Although I know that this way of thinking is stupid, I still feel a strong sense of guilt and shame. It wasn't "rape"; it was just "drunk".

Two weeks later, I came home from school to find my diary open on my bed. It had been left open on the page where I had written about what had happened to me that night. My mother had come across it while cleaning and read it all. I was horrified.

Worse still, when she sat me down to talk about it she inadvertently blamed me. She explained that she was disappointed in me that I was sexually active and although my experience was unfortunate, when alcohol is involved, bad things can happen. When girls get drunk we have a way of not being able to control our sexuality and I probably egged him on without realising it. "That's what happens when you get drunk," she explained, as if it was a perfectly normal thing to happen. The way she talked to me, her tone almost sounded as if women should expect it to happen to them when they drink too much.

My brain didn't recognise the person it was talking to. I couldn't believe that she would ever choose someone else over me. That she could read my diary, or that she could be such a coward. I had been ignored and completely disregarded by my mother. This response caused a whole new frenzied questioning in my head about what really happened that night. I further doubted myself.

Even now, I still sometimes don't believe it was rape. I find myself denying my own story. I never really speak about it in detail, even to myself.

When I think about it I feel like I'm probably overreacting and that makes me feel guilty. I am plagued by the idea that there is an acceptable definition of rape and that what happened to me does not fit this definition.

Does what happened qualify as rape? Aren't victims meant to be threatened or beaten bloody? Isn't rape usually brutal with lots of screaming and crying? In the absence of violence, wasn't it just a bad sexual experience? I mean, wasn't it me that asked for a condom in the first place? My mum seems to think that it was just alcohol and misguided feminine wiles.

These ideas that I had begun to entertain, although utterly stupid, seemed to come from all around me. The more I questioned my way of thinking, the more I realised that there was a myriad of underlying double standards and acceptable social behaviours influencing young women and men about what a woman should and shouldn't be or do, and these ideas were steering me toward blaming myself for what happened. I was a product of my culture.

The more I questioned, the more I realised that these ideas are taught in our schools and passed down through families. I quickly came to the conclusion, however unfair, that it is easier to blame the person that it happened to rather than go straight to the source and confront them with their behaviour. For those same reasons, I couldn't bring myself to be rude to my rapist. It was taught to me. I constrained myself in favour of acting appropriately. When you have no self-worth, you buy it. You willingly disenfranchise yourself for the sake of appearance and social politeness and you give away your strength because you believe that you don't deserve any better. In some cases it's because you simply don't know any better. This is how I started to think and feel about myself: powerless and insignificant.

That night, however, had only added to what was already a complicated and painful upbringing for me. I think perhaps the reason I was raped is because I was already in a self-destructive downward spiral. I allowed myself to be in a position where I would get hurt. Of course, I wasn't expecting to be raped, but I was already broken before it happened. I was trying to manifest my psychological pain into a more tangible physical pain through self-destructive outlets, which lead me further into dangerous situations.

I had an abusive father who suffered addiction and a really lovely mother who put up with it because [insert this week's preferred excuse as to why he did what he did to us]. As a family, we were always scared of setting him off. He himself suffered a very painful and traumatic childhood. In fact, he never wanted children. He loved to push buttons for the sake of the reaction and he had no problem testing out his new mind games with us whenever he fancied.

I had already written my father off as a person I could not trust very early on in my life, and had no expectations of him whatsoever. The rape had simply confirmed my suspicions about men, that they in fact do not protect you like they do in the movies, and you could only really ever rely on yourself.

My mother also had an extremely traumatic and abusive

childhood. She had become co-dependent in her relationship with my father. As a child, I had no idea, but now as I piece what I can remember together, I think I'm angrier with her than with him. She allowed him to do those things to us. The heart breaking part however was there always seemed to be some excuse as to why it wasn't his fault, or even better, why it was our fault.

There were so many times when I'd try to have a heart-to-heart with her. She would tell me that I was just being oversensitive, or that he was doing the best that he could, or that we were lucky that he wasn't a violent man like so many other families out there. I thought that the scars on my wrists would be enough to communicate to her that I was desperately unhappy, but she refused to hear. She was too scared to really hear me.

It wasn't until I was 33 years old that I realised that my mother was unable to emotionally support me. That she would always choose him instead of me.

I think at this stage I was unable to trust. I developed a very detached attitude towards people. I can be intimate and discuss very personal things about myself with anyone, but I never let anyone in. I expect to be let down so I won't put my heart into things. I can't seem to truly connect or commit, not even in friendship. On the rare occasion where a person really wants to get to know me and be a part of my life, I run for the hills.

I fear that my past choices in men are due to the fact that I am unsure what to expect from men. My father was a bully. He would humiliate me in front of his friends when they came to drink at our house, or he would treat me like a personal slave when he was too lazy to do things for himself. He would only be nice to me when he wanted something and then turn vicious when he grew tired of it. He certainly treated my mum like garbage and I see some of their behaviour now in me.

My father doesn't know who I am. He doesn't know what I like or what I've done in my life because he was never interested in me as a person. I was always just something in the house, hanging around and cutting into his drinking time. I was nothing to him and I felt like I was nothing but for some reason I always tried so hard to get him to love me. Each time I was denied.

I think the lack of having a positive father figure in my life had already skewed my view about love, affection and my view about myself. Love for me at that time was only granted when I was deemed worthy by him, like a dog doing tricks for treats.

After the rape, it skewed my view further about the sexes and my own self-worth. I didn't see the equality I learned about in school. Women, in my new awakened reality, were definitely being portrayed and treated negatively in almost every facet of society and culture that I could see. And women that were deemed to be a certain type were treated like trash. I saw the difference in the way I was treated compared to other girls. This made me very angry.

Growing up, I never really liked myself much but it wasn't until I was raped that I truly hated being a woman. In fact, I still resent being a woman. I feel trapped by the expectations of my sex. I feel that as a woman, my only worth is in my looks. I am the receiver, whether I want to receive or not. My job is sex because I have a vagina. I see women all around the world being used like a commodity, a thing; bought and sold. To a certain degree our culture still accepts and supports these concepts by turning a blind eye or accepting the lesser evil rather than doing what's right. It's in our advertising, magazines and TV. Women themselves at times support some of these notions without realising it, because it is ingrained in us that it is acceptable.

I'm aware that a healthy sexual relationship is founded on love and trust but my thoughts about sex and the sexes have caused me to disconnect from the act itself. Sex to me is more of a performance. As long as I make the right noises in the appropriate places, it doesn't matter how I really feel. Sex is about him not me. I'm just a body. In reality, I don't get anything from sex. It doesn't feel good to me. Sometimes I think that maybe if it did feel good for me, perhaps psychologically, what happened to me that night wouldn't bother me as much and I would be able to move on. But I find sex humiliating. Being a woman for me is humiliating.

After that night, I shut my heart. My beliefs were unhinged, my trust disintegrated and my core functionalities that make a healthy human being were replaced by fear, hatred and self-degradation. For a very long time after that I cultivated dysfunctional behaviours to cope with all the questions in my head about myself and why it happened. It especially heightened my sense of worthlessness.

The painful part of all of this is that I want to love with everything that I have. I want to trust people and be brave but I will not allow myself to let go. I cannot reprogram. Recognising these things in myself however, has finally made me realise that I am the only one who has the power to help myself.

My actions were questionable that night and I was reckless, but he made the choice to hurt me. What he did reflects more on his nature than mine. I need to push past my own humiliation, forget about what people may or may not be thinking or saying about me and stop being so hard on myself. What I experienced that night may not have been the textbook definition of rape, if there is even such a thing, but it was no less horrifying or humiliating. That boy had forced himself into me unwelcomed, without regard. He left me there when he was done, like I was rubbish. But I need to remember that these were his decisions, his choices, not mine.

I'm sure reliving it over and over in my mind will never go away but my choice is to stop taking responsibility for his shame unto myself. I'm not proud of drinking myself unconscious and it was my responsibility to look after myself better but I didn't force myself onto a drunk person and take advantage of them and I need to stop blaming myself for everything that happened that night.

I now know that I am the common denominator in my life. I'm the problem but also the solution. Looking at my past, my issues with family were an unfortunate false start in life for me. In all fairness, I'm sure that my parents tried to do the best they could.

By trying to cope with the pain of rejection and abandonment in my family life, I turned to self-harm through alcohol and reckless behaviour. These behaviours bore consequences. My choices brought people into my life that used or hurt me. This caused me to retreat further into myself and away from the world which has hurt me in other ways. The fact that I have been raped exacerbates these pre-existing issues I carry. It also gave me an excuse to give up.

I'm now on a journey to try to change the way I live and think.

My choices and actions can take me to better places. I need to be strong, truthful, but most of all responsible for what I say and do, even when I have behaved badly. If I can be truthful to myself and accept the weak and not-so-nice parts of me too, then nothing can ever hurt me.

Currently, I work in a secure, well-paying position where I have established strong networks and good working relationships. I have invited good people into my life who really care about me and I, in turn, care about them – people who actually want to see me be happy. Good people who actively help me succeed in the things I pursue on a daily basis. People who have helped me believe in myself again and allowed me to dream bigger and better things for myself.

I have been studying web and app development to diversify my skill set so that I may be able to better understand e-business. One day, I hope to start my own online store to showcase the creative aspirations that were once so painful for me to express or explore. It will be hard but I think this will be a positive challenge for me. I am no longer afraid of failing.

My biggest achievement so far however is the purchase of my first apartment. This is something that I have always wanted, and although I feel supercilious to say so, I have managed to do it on my own. This unit is my "base". Having a place that I can call my own was always important to me. The saying "home is where the heart is" is true for me. It is here that I have been able to rebuild myself and make new goals.

In three months, I will have the finances to purchase my second property. My long-term goal is to own enough property to allow me to retire early so that I may be able to pursue further education in the arts. I have somehow enabled and renewed my drive. I have strengthened my will to continue on a less destructive path. I have not given up on trying.

I'm pretty sure that I'm still broken and very certain I'm still a long way off from brilliant, but I'm getting closer to making peace with myself and knowing my own mind. I'm trying not to be so hard on myself. I am facing the more confronting things in life head-on without telling lies, accepting lies or turning a blind eye. I'm retraining myself to articulate and clearly communicate what I want without apology. I aspire to live as a good person, the person I want to be rather than what may be expected of me. I want to be the best I can be. I know now, that is really all I can be.

And that is OK, because I am enough.

Be the best you, your way

You are valuable and have unique gifts. Bring out the best brilliant you for the world to see.

- YOUR CHOICE: Know you have chosen where you are in your life. You can choose to change it if it is not what you want and you are not free to be who you want.
- YOUR RIGHT: Saying No or Stop is okay and is not rude or impolite, it's your right.
- YOUR KNOWLEDGE: Know and tell others that force against another's will is abuse, forcing sex on someone is rape and we all have a responsibility to ensure others are safe, supported and not abused.
- YOUR STRENGTH: Don't take part in activities for the sake of appearance, peer pressure or social politeness – you give away your strength, soul and yourself.
- YOUR VOICE: Clearly and respectfully articulate and communicate what you want and do not want.
- YOUR INVITATION: Invite and accept good people into your life – people who want to help you with your dreams and to succeed, those who make you feel good about yourself.
- YOUR FUTURE: Start studying something you are interested in and diversify your skill set.
- YOUR LESSONS: Embrace and learn from all experiences, good and bad, and come back stronger and smarter.
- YOUR ASPIRATIONS: Have aspirations, set short and long-term goals and continually work towards them.
- YOUR WINS: Celebrate all achievements.

© Broken to Brilliant

CHAPTER FIVE

TEARS AND TIME

"Look back on all of the past events and believe that they have helped to make you the special woman that you are today."

I STILL REMEMBER SO CLEARLY MY FEELINGS OF LOSS AND EMPTIness as I was discharged from hospital. There in the car park outside the hospital, I sat in my little car with an odd anger towards my psychiatrist for sending me away, while in my head screaming that I wasn't ready to leave. I didn't know what to do, how to live or even why I should live. You see, the only reason I was still living was the promise I had made to my parents that I would go on living, and I always keep my promises. Even though my father has now died, my mother is still very much alive, and I still keep the promise to them both.

As I drove away from the hospital, where I had been for almost eight weeks, I remember the feelings of emptiness and loss. In this car, I had most of the things I needed to go forward in my life apart from my dogs, and the hospital had been home to me, my place of sanctuary.

I never actually tried to take my life, but I was intending to. I had the means all ready and had written the suicide notes in such a small scratchy way, but my body (or the universe) stopped me by becoming almost catatonic – I could hardly think or move. I felt like I was too heavy to move, it was too hard to lift my arm. As the weeks progressed I realised I had lost my sense of smell along with the will to live. Yes, at this time I wanted to die.

My parents were totally unprepared for my depression because I was seen as the strong one in the family. To date, I'm the first and only one of my family to have been divorced. When I married I committed to a long-term relationship which I took very seriously. It was a lifelong commitment for good or bad, but to have the man I was married to wanting (and being with) men, not me, was too much. The long-term relationship had to end.

You see I went from having a family, children, a home, a life (bad as it was for me) and a long-term relationship to having nothing. I didn't know my purpose: Why am I here? What am I to do?

It seemed to me that it happened all in one day, though in reality it was a week or two. Some events of that time are cloudy for me, which may be a protective device! Then there was also the workplace bullying I was experiencing from above, below and laterally! You see my partner and I worked together.

The importance of a life purpose was so big for me. I had to have a reason to go on. When I left the hospital I was only hanging on for my parents. I had made a promise and I always keep my promises.

I didn't have a physically violent relationship; it fell into the category of manipulation and psychological abuse. I just couldn't take the negative poisonous home life anymore. Something had to change. Then I discovered my partner of many years was gay.

How did I find out?

I shared my story of life events as best I could recall with a legal official. They said, "From your story today, as your partner hasn't been intimate with you since the conception of your youngest child over ten years ago and you're not an unattractive woman – who could he be having relations with?"

After hearing my whole story the reply was, "It sounds like your partner is gay."

Wow! Open curtains! I saw fireworks in my mind. Yes, this makes sense, but why have I not seen this before?

I'd seen a communication between work colleagues that hadn't made sense. "I'll always be there for the children."

Another of our colleagues saw me around this time and asked if I was all right, because I didn't look okay. I replied, "No, I think my relationship is over."

Their response was, "I'm not surprised. We all wondered how much longer it would be. We all know." I couldn't reply, I was dumbfounded – obviously the last to know. They say the wife is usually the last to know.

The legal official told me I needed to get money together – a "fighting fund" – which I did by moving money in our shared accounts, something I'd never have dreamed of doing before this conversation. I had never been allowed to have savings – money was always spent on things that were great but they were never for me, a new car, a new computer or new luggage etc. – and I didn't have any private savings.

My partner told me that money over $5,000 could not be moved from our accounts – I found out it was a lie! There were more lies, too. I had been waiting on financial letters, then I found letters addressed to me, hidden away. I wonder who could have possibly put them there! There was an arrangement that he would contribute the maximum to super and we would live from my pay. Stupid, or too trusting? Anyway, that is in the past.

I experienced being blamed for many things and psychological manipulation. After a number of years of abstinence I broached the subject as to why we didn't make love anymore. There were tears, and the alleged impotence, and all of it was my fault as I'd made him have a vasectomy. Later, I asked why we didn't cuddle and kiss anymore. The response was that it was a reminder that "it" – pointing to his penis – didn't work anymore. By now, I was seeking help from the medical community; I was sad and depressed all the time.

I thought that his work took him away from home a lot. When people asked where he was I'd say, "Oh, he's on secret men's business!" It seems so funny now, looking back, but I really didn't know what he was doing as he gave me so many different stories. He'd be gone and too often I'd run out of money because he'd taken what he needed from our joint accounts. Then I would have to borrow from my youngest child to buy milk and bread.

When he would come home, the children and I didn't want to hear about the great foods he'd had or the special places he'd been to – we were sick of it. We were left behind; alone we had to deal with the difficulties of work/life balance, the challenges of adolescence, just to name a few issues. We grew to be a different family while he was away. Then he'd come home and impose his way on us. My skills as mother, full-time worker and single parent were always being criticised and worst of all, I was always criticised in front of the children. Looking back, no wonder I had problems with the children growing up. I was struggling to just survive, while being constantly put down. I was criticised for everything I did – nothing was good enough. This was going on at home and work.

There was so much control over me that I wasn't allowed – yes I said "wasn't allowed" – to have my own credit card, let alone bank accounts! One day I was in a shop with my eldest child buying clothes for the school formal when he called me on the mobile and said, "What the bloody hell are you spending $120 on?" Yes, my spending was being tracked! It wasn't even for me but for our child.

A few years later I received a letter offering me a credit card and luckily I took the offer, as this started to give me an individual credit rating, which I would later need. He was ropeable to discover it one night when he opened my mail – "by accident" he said. He came into my bedroom (we were now sleeping apart) and in front of our youngest child accused me of stealing from the relationship, as I now had a credit card in my name. From that day until we separated, I had to buy all the food for the family and clothes for me and the children from my own accounts. Having my own financial independence did not go down well. At every opportunity I was put down in front of our own children.

People have often asked me why I didn't know he was gay. Well, I had been a so-called "good" girl, and I had no other experiences with which to compare my relationship. It is only recently that I have found women who would openly discuss sex and intimacy with me. A couple of years after my relationship breakup, I took myself into a sex store and bought some sex education videos. That was embarrassing at fifty years of age, but I had to learn. What a journey!

Looking back, I believe I would have been able to cope, if I had not lost everything. But I lost my children, my family life, my friends, my partner and my career. So when everything I thought I had was taken away and over thirty years of life was found to be nothing but a lie, my self-esteem was shattered. My children had gone with him.

The day after we settled our financial affairs, I got a call from a government agency to tell me I now had to pay child support for my youngest. During our relationship, he would on occasion say, "Our relationship is over." This would come unexpectedly, usually when we had travelled to visit my parents. He never explained why, just that it was over. Then a day later he'd recant, and to him all was fine. Talk about confusing and cruel. I didn't know what to do or who to talk with.

For twenty odd years of the relationship I'd always put his career needs first and mine second. It ended when I asked for a trial separation, using a note I put on his pillow in his private den. To this day, I do not know where this energy to ask for action came from.

I had a friend put a key lock on my bedroom door, as I was feeling very unsafe at that time. There were lots of things happening that made me feel unsafe. Money was going missing, jewellery too, and I was being blamed for bank accounts being overdrawn, but mostly I know now I was feeling unsafe psychologically.

At work, I felt this was organised so that I felt isolated from my peer group, and whatever else I'll never know and do not care to know now. But the staff at work knew there was a choice, they had to keep their jobs. I knew this was only part of the manipulation he was capable of.

All I ever wanted was to be at home as much as possible for our children, but I wasn't allowed to be a stay-at-home parent, I had to work. So I was always looking for work that allowed me to be there for my children as much as possible. My mum had gone to work when I was about eight years old and I hated it – we were latchkey kids. I was the eldest of three, with the key and all the responsibility to look after my sister and brother, and get tea started for mum. I was never able to do any after school activities as a child because Mum worked and dad was a shift worker. Like most parents, I wanted much more for my children.

When our children chose to go with him, it tore me apart. So there I was depressed and getting worse, I didn't know where my children were or how to contact them, I was being bullied at work and there was no purpose to life. I missed my kids terribly but I knew I wasn't going to be allowed to have them; such skilful manipulation. My parents and legal official believed the manipulation was pushing me to kill myself. No sharing, just get me out of the way.

After my relationship breakup, I experienced a lot more workplace bullying. I eventually left my employers with a large payout, and no confidentiality contract. According to my union adviser, this was unheard of.

It's now over a decade later and I am living a totally different life. I have discovered how to love again, but am still broken hearted that I'm estranged from my children and I still do not know why.

When I left school, I studied and achieved a number of qualifications. I loved working in three states of Australia and was fortunate to work in many varied areas over nearly forty years, but when my back became too painful and surgery could not stop the pain I had to give up my career.

It was not until I had retired that I realised how much of my identity centred around who I was in my career. With this I had to deal with another loss.

This has been exceptionally hard to deal with as I loved my chosen career path and always did. I still miss being able to help people through my skills and wondered what was to fill my life now? Then my father died and my young niece was tragically killed – more losses to bear.

Over recent years, I have spent a lot of time with a wonderful psychiatrist; I have tried many antidepressants with their many side effects. I have a fantastic relationship with my new general practitioner (GP). The GP I had been seeing during my relationship and immediately after the breakup failed to see how depressed I was. I make this point because I had sought help for my depression but the medical system didn't understand at the time how sick I was. Today I hope there's a better understanding, but if you know someone who may be in need of help I implore you to reach out and help them.

I have dealt with breast cancer, with the hot flashes and power bursts from menopause, where my blood pressure would skyrocket, and endured many other nasty symptoms.

No-one really knows what goes on behind closed doors. Never assume that a person's life is perfect. Other people – even my parents until the last year or so of my life with my partner – thought my life was happy. Except that my mother said to me once that it was heart breaking to see the light going out of my eyes, she wanted to see me return – by that she explained she wanted to see the enthusiastic intelligent woman she had known return, with all her spunk and cheekiness.

No-one in my family of origin and all the extensions has seen my children since the relationship broke up. My father went to his grave wondering why they went away, and it hurt.

Thinking back as I have been writing this chapter, the real key to my moving from despair to where I am today has been my search for peace and my goal to live in the moment. I chose to change my way of thinking. I chose to move forward in a positive way. I consciously chose to do this in my daily language and in the words I used when journaling.

I choose not to knock myself on the head if and when I need a good cry. In fact, I often schedule a crying session, to allow me to empty my bucket of sadness in a controlled way. I would recommend a good cry at a time and place that is safe. Crying is very therapeutic. It's like so many sad memories or thoughts go into a bucket and the bucket needs planned emptying or it will start to spill out at unexpected times and places.

I have learnt how to be a life coach, mostly to help myself; I have participated in many seminars and courses trying to find a new purpose. I have read self-improvement books and cried. Oh how I have cried! I have written a journal and meditated.

Now I choose to think positively. I look back on all of the past events and believe that they have helped to make me the special woman that I am today. You see, I am a glass-half-full type of person.

An unexpected by-product of my sadness was the feelings of repulsion it generated around me. People saw me as an angry and negative person. This was for me a very bad perception, as I was lonely and seeking out people for friendship. Who would choose to be friends with a negative, angry, hurt person? Not even me!

I now choose to live in peace, in the moment, in a joyous positive way and firstly to love myself.

I had to change my thinking not for others' sake but for mine! I believe that soon my children and I will reunite, as it should be with mothers and their children.

I have dabbled successfully in property development and renovations, and am currently completing the process to become a Justice of the Peace (Qualified). I believe in giving back to one's community and this is why I am becoming a JP. I also take every opportunity I can get to meet new people, learn new skills, and often add to my growing list of friends.

When I was asked what helped me most, the answer is: me and roughly ten years of time. So hang in there ladies. It's not impossible to survive – and not only to survive but also to become exceptional. When I was approached about being in this book, I didn't hesitate because that is who I am – a helper. I hope that by sharing some of my story it can help other women dealing with some of the worst life has to offer.

It's only after putting my story on paper that I have realised the emotional abuse that I lived through and its effects, which rear their ugly heads repeatedly. I want people to identify as early as possible when you are in this type of relationship. I have attended a lot of courses and conferences and worked on my inner self, but this process of telling my story has been very therapeutic.

By the way, I don't hate my ex-partner, this would only hurt me and I choose not to be hurt anymore. I choose to be happy and hopeful and make every day count in a positive way. I believe I will be reconnected with my children – this I truly believe.

Wishing you all health and happiness.

Time HELPS to ARMOUR

Healthcare	Seek help from health professionals. If feel you are not getting the help you need, find a health professional who understands your situation.	
Education	Attend seminars, workshops and education sessions, read self-improvement books .	
Live Now	Focus on living in the moment. Do not look back and do not look forward, focus on the precious present.	
Peace	Search for peace – meditate.	
Self	Keep the light in your eyes flickering – if your inner light is fading you are not living a life true to yourself.	
Attitude	Change the way you think. Move forward in a positive way; be positive in the language you use and your journaling.	
Reflect	Look at the events of your life in a different way – to me they have been character building.	
Money	Always have your own money – private savings for financial security and independence.	
OUtpouring	Fill your bucket with tears – have a good cry, don't beat yourself up for it. But do not wallow in sadness either – empty the bucket and move on.	
Repay	Give back to others and the community.	

© Broken to Brilliant

CHAPTER SIX

THE BADGE OF SUFFERING

"I changed my victim mentality to one of empowerment, confidence and internal happiness."

I WAS AN ONLY CHILD FOR ALMOST FIVE YEARS — BY ALL ACCOUNTS a spoilt only child. I was my Daddy's little girl – the firstborn child of Catholic migrants.

One of my earliest memories is of standing in a hospital room, holding my father's hand and looking at my mother and my new baby brother. I don't recall feeling anything negative about the situation at this stage, but that would soon change drastically.

When my new brother was only a few days old, my teddy bear was taken from me and given to him. I was two months away from my fifth birthday and deemed "too old" for a teddy. This teddy had been given to me by Father Christmas and I was very attached to him. He was almost as big as I was and made of mohair with jointed limbs. I did not react well to having my bear taken from me, showing my displeasure by kicking and screaming and crying and begging to be given back my bear. I remember the feelings of outrage and grief very clearly. When my teddy left, it felt like the love went with him.

I was inconsolable and outraged for what must have been

quite a long time. Eventually my parents (probably to shut me up) bought a cheap little panda bear and gave it to me. I wanted my own bear back but he now belonged to my brother. That's when the resentment towards my brother began. We lived in a two-bedroom house and when my brother was about a year old, he was given my bedroom and I was made to sleep in the dining room on a fold-up bed.

As we grew up and another girl joined the family, my brother continued to be the preferred child. He created havoc for my sister because she was a lot younger than him. He excelled at setting her up to get into trouble, and he never incurred the wrath of our parents, no matter what he did. I was forced to play with him; I couldn't play with my friends unless I had spent time with him first.

I spent a large part of my childhood locked in a room, kicking and screaming, and the other part, scrubbing the black marks off the door.

For my twenty-first birthday, I received a card. My sister received half the price of a food processor. Our brother received a party and a state of the art stereo.

As a teenager, I was very rebellious and my parents were ridiculously strict. At the age of eighteen I was allowed out one night a week and had to be home at midnight. If I came home at ten minutes past twelve, my father would be sitting outside on the wall in his pyjamas and would hurl abuse at me and whomever I was with.

After a particularly unpleasant session of abuse, which carried on into the Sunday, I decided I'd had enough and that it was time to leave home. I packed up my multiple pairs of shoes and their matching handbags, as well as my clothes and toiletries and headed off. My brother and sister were hanging off my legs and my mother was in tears, begging me to stay. My father was adamant that it was his house and they were his rules and if I didn't like it, I could leave.

I didn't really have anywhere to go, so I moved in with the young man I had been going out with for three weeks. He was part of the latest argument with my father, having delivered me home ten minutes late the previous night.

At that time, it was very difficult to get the birth control pill unless you were married, so of course, a couple of months later, I was pregnant. We moved from one state to another and despite being under 20 years of age, I became a mother and I was all alone. I knew no-one except for the father of my child and he was less than wonderful. Labour had to be induced. On the day I was to go into hospital, he had an event to attend, so he lined up one of his mates, whom I had never met, to take me to the hospital. Luckily, the mate was a bit older and I think he felt sorry for me. He was very kind and considerate.

The relationship was not good. I hated this man for getting me pregnant and he hated me for getting pregnant. In addition, because of his own upbringing, he hated women. He was not physically abusive but, just like my parents, he was emotionally abusive and also sadistic, not just to me but to our son. This was the cause of a great deal of friction and arguments as I tried to protect my little boy.

We came back down to the same city where my family lived,

but my parents wouldn't let him in the house. I told them we were a family now and if they wouldn't accept him, they were not accepting their daughter and their grandson either. I didn't see them for a few months and then my father tracked us down and made peace again.

We bought a caravan and travelled up and down the coast of Australia for a few years. While we were on the road, we weren't allowed to stop for a drink or a toilet break because we had to be "toughened up". He would drive well into the night and then sleep half the day. This meant that my sleep routine was completely ruined and I still suffer from poor sleep to this day. During this time, we had an accident and rolled the caravan. Luckily we weren't injured but it was very stressful. The caravan was written off and we had to buy another. There was never any compassion or softness shown towards me. We fought constantly and I was miserable.

After years of continual arguing, name calling, carping and not being allowed to spend one cent without permission, I summoned up the courage to leave him. I rented a house with my son, thirty kilometres from where we had purchased our first home.

Not long after we left, it was Father's Day. I felt sorry for my ex, so I allowed him to have my son for the weekend. When it was time for me to collect him, he wouldn't give him back. A court hearing was booked and the night before the hearing, my ex turned up at my house in the middle of the night, with our son, the dog and all sorts of household goods loaded into the back of the ute. He said that unless I withdrew my claim for custody, he would take our son on the run. We went to court the next day and my barrister and the judge were very concerned that I had withdrawn my custody claim. (In those days, the woman nearly always got custody.) I told them what had happened to cause me to withdraw my custody claim and my ex denied everything. The judge offered to lock him up but I knew he would come and take our son as soon as he was free. I knew that unless he was locked up for the next sixteen years, I would lose my son.

He promised he would return our son to school, with his friends. In the interests of my son being able to stay in his familiar surroundings and at the same school, I reluctantly agreed to the terms. Less than two years later, they had left the country on a false passport and he stayed away for two years. I had no idea where they were. Every so often my parents would receive a postcard from China or some other place, as a teaser, but we never had an address.

Eventually, after two years, they came home. My son wanted to come and live with me. I had another relationship and another child, and was living in a different city. My son moved in with us. He could barely speak English. They had lived overseas and now my son only spoke the same non-English language of my parent's heritage. Luckily so did I, so it wasn't a huge problem at home. He went to school and relearned English over a few months. He struggled with the structure of our lives as he had been allowed total freedom. I did what I thought was appropriate for an eleven year old boy but it was too restrictive for him and he went back to his father after a year. I saw my eldest son fairly regularly after that as we moved back to the same city we grew up in and where he was living.

I believed in my next relationship I had found my soul mate, but after fourteen and a half years I discovered he had been cheating on me from day one. So another relationship bit the dust! It nearly killed me. I struggled with serious depression and suicidal thoughts. I lost almost ten kilograms in a week and my clothes literally fell off me. One morning, I put on my jeans, did them up and they fell to the floor. I'm all in favour of losing weight but not like that!

After three years of financial and emotional struggle, trying to work part time and provide a normal life for my son, I met a different man altogether – my present partner. He is good and kind and caring and we have been together for more than twenty years.

About fifteen years ago, I started having severe pain in my legs and was constantly struggling to do the simplest things. I had muscle tests, bone tests and nerve tests. Everything came back as normal, yet I was in excruciating pain. It moved all over my legs and changed from sharp pains to a dull ache, to throbbing, seemingly at random. I was eventually diagnosed with fibromyalgia. I tried many things to try to ease the pain but nothing worked. After a few years, we were forced to sell our dream home because I couldn't climb the stairs. I couldn't stand for more than a minute and I had a walking stick and occasionally a wheelchair. I thought I would be crippled for life.

I am an ex specialist nurse and qualified in natural therapies and had over the years come to specialise in helping people with depression and anxiety. About seven years ago, I had a new client who was in a bad way. She was very depressed and suicidal. I did what I had always done in these cases – kinesiology and Bach Flower therapy – but it wasn't working. She kept coming back and she was getting worse. This had never happened to me before. My clients always got better, quite quickly. I feared for her life. In desperation, I started looking for something else that may help her.

We've all heard the expression that "the universe provides" and so it did. I received an email inviting me to a free three-day seminar and, although it didn't specify what it was about, it sounded as though it would give me what I was looking for. I called my client and told her I was going to the seminar to learn how to help her. I duly went off and it turned out the seminar was all about this thing called Neuro Linguistic Programming (NLP). It was an incredible weekend and I maxed out my credit card to go and do the first two lots of training.

Unfortunately, there were months until the first training commenced. I had to keep a very close watch on my client and keep reassuring her that I would be able to help her soon.

The first lot of training eventually came about – seven extremely long, consecutive days. It was gruelling and at the end I felt as though I had been run over by a bus.

As soon as I got home, I called my client in. I spent about three hours with her, utilising all that I had learned, all the while fumbling through the manual and being unsure and a little wooden. In spite of these limitations, she came out of the session in a wonderful state of mind, feeling better than she had for years. I occasionally see her around and she has never gone back to that awful place of deep despair and suicidal thoughts.

My father had been dead for many years by then, but just prior to the first training, I had a huge argument with my family. There was an 83rd birthday party being organised on the same weekend of the first training, which started on a Sunday. I said I could come on the Saturday but not on the Sunday. They were unable to get the venue for the Saturday so booked it for the Sunday instead. I paid my share, did my share of the cooking but I made it very clear that I would not be attending. Another member of my family was also doing the course so they didn't go either. The relative whose birthday I did not attend was furious with me and I'm sure she didn't ever forgive me.

Three weeks later, she died and left me an inheritance.

The fact that I had been left money meant that I could continue my studies. I did the next gruelling seven-day training later in the year, and continued studying for a period of twelve months.

During this time, we students practised on one another, working through all of our issues, steadily and profoundly. Many of the training exercises were done while standing for up to half an hour or more. I always had to sit on a chair.

I was brought up to believe that life is hard and unfair – they were my mother's almost final words – and that "people like us" didn't have money. I learned to believe that everything is a struggle and there is very little joy. Well into my late 50s I still believed that categorically. I didn't know there was any other way to think. Sadly, I also passed that mindset onto my children.

As I came to the end of the training, I started to see that there are other perspectives and that life can be easy and happy and comfortable. This was a revelation to me. I embraced it fully, and diligently continued to work on all my issues of anger and resentment about my upbringing, my parents' withdrawal of love and my life experiences. In fact, I changed my victim mentality to one of empowerment and confidence and internal happiness.

Also, as I came to the end of my training, I realised that I no longer had any pain in my legs. I could stand for a period of time, I could climb stairs and I was pain free for the first time in about fifteen years. The fibromyalgia was my "badge of suffering" – "look what they've done to me". When I no longer needed to be defined by my past, I could let that badge of suffering go and be a happier and more positive version of myself. I also no longer collect teddy bears and have even started to give some of them away!

The beautiful thing about this story is that the person who was the cause of my problem also gave me the means to overcome the problem. My spiritual beliefs tell me that I made a contract with my family members, before we incarnated. We agreed that they would be a certain way and I would be a certain way, so we could all learn from one another and, hopefully, learn our life lessons. We made this contract out of the deep love we all have for one another. I now fully embrace that understanding and thank my family for being who they were in my life and for ultimately giving me the means to take a giant leap forwards in my life. I truly honour them for that gift.

These days, I work as a Life Coach using a range of therapies and my greatest joy is seeing my clients leave my consulting room inspired and empowered, no longer victims of their past, but masters of their own destiny.

I have heard many hideous and heart-rending stories over the years but the really great news is that no matter what your story is, no matter how tragic – it is not you! You are more than your story, very much more, and you *do* have what it takes to rebuild your life, your self-esteem and your confidence.

I found it quite uncomfortable trawling through my past for this chapter because I don't focus on those things anymore. They are no longer who I am. If my story can help anyone, then I've sat in the discomfort for a good cause.

What badge are you wearing?

Take a look at what badge you are wearing.
- Do you blame someone else?
- Do you think or talk about how badly-done-by you are?
- Does one person always make you feel bad?
- Does your head say "look what they have done to me"?

If you answered yes to any of the above questions you have a "blame others" attitude. This is the warning sign that you are wearing a badge of suffering.

A different badge to wear

1. **Love your life lessons.** Your story is not you. Look at your life events as lessons in life and have gratitude for these experiences – this will change your mindset.

2. **Want lifelong returns.** Invest in education – take courses that can change your life psychologically and physically.

3. **Take action now.** Implement what you have learned straight away, as it takes 3–9 months to make a behavioural change – don't waste a minute.
   - Do not focus on the past – this keeps you in a victim mode.
   - Your attitudes, beliefs and perspectives are your choice.
   - Change your beliefs if they don't serve you.
   - See other perspectives – life can be easy, happy and comfortable.
   - Change your victim mentality to one of empowerment, confidence and internal happiness.

© Broken to Brilliant

CHAPTER SEVEN

GENUINE HUMAN KINDNESS CAN CHANGE YOUR LIFE

"You are smart, brilliant and never broken. You don't need to be fixed and nobody can take what you don't give them. Own your brilliance, own your power and own your radiance. Once awakened, acknowledged and embraced, it is yours forever."

HUMAN KINDNESS. WHAT DOES THIS MEAN AND WHAT CAN IT DO for one person? For me it was everything. One Saturday afternoon, they lifted me from beneath the bushes, pulled leaves out of my hair, dusted the dirt off my shoulders and then strapped me to an ambulance gurney. I will never forget that day. When they all pooled together and bought me a present to thank me… well, then I was blown away.

I married young; I had not even reached 20 years of age, psychologically I was about 16 considering my smothering upbringing. In retrospect, getting married was a crazy idea, but being young and running from my upbringing's clutches, I guess it made sense.

A male family member was extremely possessive and controlling of me. He used to tell me that I couldn't sleep over at my friend's or even my cousin's house because someone might put something in my drink and take advantage of me. So I hardly got to go anywhere.

The truth of the matter was, this man was the one abusing me! Sexual molestation and emotional confusion were at the helm of our relationship. From my earliest memory, it was his behaviour that kept me in a prison of shame. Since this was all I knew, I didn't understand another way. I "adored" him. I was "special". I was the one that he would take to adult parties and I was the one he wanted sitting next to him at home or in the car or anywhere. It was me.

He qualified everything I was and everything I needed to be, to be loved and feel loved. Even though he was explosive and demeaning, I learned to believe that I just had to be a "good girl", look pretty and behave, never talk back or put up a fight. This would keep the peace.

His anger and frustration, which would turn into insults and emotional attacks, were always directed to other family members. There was this gut-wrenching pain in my soul as I would watch with regret and sorrow the pain that was inflicted on my family members because of my actions to fight him off. It was them that would suffer. So time and time again, I would comply with his demands. Remembering the tears and the almost fistfights he and my family would get into, I felt responsible. It became so overwhelming that I started to shut myself down.

The radiant part of my soul was hidden, buried underneath a surreal wall of protection. My light darkened, my voice silenced, and my life felt like an illusion.

At 18, I rebelled. I was determined to do anything to be out of my home. I figured, "I am 18. I can do whatever I want and you can't stop me!"

I would be told, "Be back home at 10", so I would be back at 12. When told I couldn't go somewhere, I would just leave.

I met a lady who was 21 and worked at a bar, so she became my close friend. After all, she could buy me drinks and I could escape mentally. Funny how warped our thinking becomes when under the surreal spell of salvation and self-mutilation. I would go out night after night and hang out until all hours of the night with my girlfriend and some friends. My girlfriend had her own place so it was just the environment I needed to escape.

When a male friend left the services, he would join us at my girlfriend's house. He was also 21. He was funny. His smile made me feel I knew him beyond his words, beyond his tall very manly appearance. He made me laugh. He had a way about him that took me away mentally from the reality of my enduring pain back home. We were instant friends with a connection that neither one of us understood at that moment. As we got to know each other we would share things. I felt a comfort with him and I believe he felt safe with me. Then one day after a Christmas party at my girlfriend's bar, he walked me to my car and kissed me. I didn't remember the drive home that night – I was on a cloud. From that moment on there was no denying that there was something more between us.

One night when he became angered by my father, he acknowledged that my abuser's behaviour was that of a jealous man, not an angry family member. He was the first one, ever, to bring up the BIG FAT elephant in the house! This statement opened up Pandora's box!

I don't think he was ready to hear what came out of my mouth in an avalanche of tears for the next two hours. I said probably more than he needed to hear. *No-one* up to that point had ever spoken or taken notice of what was going on in my home. And then… he loved me anyway. I decided that I couldn't take it anymore; I was going to get out!

Now we were inevitably connected. I was for the first time in a world where love was unconditional and I wasn't judged for the dirtiness of my life. Or at least that was how it felt at the time. The shame that I carried was so deep that I didn't even recognize it. In my home, we had to live by a specific rule that would plague me for the rest of my time there. It was the "what will they say" rule. Everything we lived by and how we behaved had to fall under this rule. So the absolute "must" in my family home was to paint the pretty picture. The secrecy and incredibly loud silence coupled with the shame and guilt were enough to create a living hell of apathetic behaviour.

That day when I met that male friend I suddenly had a shimmer of light in my life. Through all that was going on in my life, he still wanted me, loved me, and wanted to rescue me. We would talk for hours about everything, deep things, dreams, a fairy-tale future of a family, the white picket fence and the dog. Together we were going to create a fantasy life and we believed we could and would do it. Within six months of falling in love, all I wanted to do was to be with him. I would drive an hour away just to stay with him in his apartment.

Throughout the week I would daydream about being with him and couldn't wait. I was so in love.

Meanwhile, I was still fighting off my abuser at home. Now that I had a lover and a man in my life the abuser's behaviour was worse. He was competitive and would corner me when my family was away. I felt so weak and powerless, it was crazy-making. I would hide in my room only to be yelled at for locking my door!

I couldn't take it anymore. I told my family I was moving out and that I was moving in with my boyfriend. Since the rule was, "What will 'they' say?" my family was riddled with shame and said, "Well if you are in love that much, you should get married." I was still under 20 and at this stage of my life wanted to escape my abuser and be as far away as I could. With the immense love I felt at that time for my boyfriend, it was perfect that we should get married. We didn't have the money, so my family paid for everything including our wedding rings! I moved out Monday; by Friday I was married by a justice of the peace.

It was bliss and there was passion, connection, laughter and a bond that I had never felt before. There was also a ton of insecurity. I noticed his fits of anger when small things happened, like he couldn't find a comb. I would scramble to find it or look everywhere for a replacement. His anger was coupled with vulgarity and accusations. No matter what happened, I was the one who said "Sorry".

As the years progressed, his anger got worse and worse. The emotional torment was filthy and filled with gut-wrenching words and fits of rage. Vulgarity and insults were at the core, along with jealousy, accusations, threats of suicide and bullying.

However, there was also a deep intense love, or what love looked like and felt like to me. It's what made it so confusing and what made me forgive and forgive and forgive, every time. I remember being told never to let anyone take advantage of me. But, it was never safe. The feeling was how I would imagine being in the Vietnam War... walking through the jungle never knowing if you were going to step on a landmine.

There were days that were beautiful and I remember thinking, "If you could only stay this way, things would be great. I could love you and even be intimate with you." But it never lasted. Inevitably, something would go wrong.

After having kids, there were more reasons to be stressed. His fits of rage came for all kinds of reasons, from the kids leaving a coke can on the counter, there being a stain on the shirt I laid out for him to wear, or I didn't have an ingredient that I needed for dinner. Something or someone would cause the night to shift from laughter and bonding to cuss words, insults and intimidation. I became comfortably numb. A walking, breathing, physical body without direction.

There was something inside of me that was gone. My life felt surreal, like it was floating along and I was unconscious. I wasn't suicidal because I had my kids, so that was not an option. But, I used to think, "If a car blew through the red light and hit me, maybe I could die and that would be okay." I didn't care. So I continued with life at our house and put on the face of "everything is okay". After all, I didn't want my kids to know or for them to be yelled at either.

Throughout all of this, I wanted something more in my life.

I was looking for purpose. There had to be more than this. So I signed up for Emergency Medicine Training. Since my husband was in the services, I had seen life behind the yellow tape for fourteen years and wanted the ability to help. I knew I could never be in the services so emergency medicine training seemed like the perfect fit, as I would be helping people. Taking the course introduced me to what the front line would be like.

During this course, I met a lot of people and I was terrified. I was in fear that my husband would get jealous if my study group had any males in it. Our instructor indicated that the course was a difficult one and that group study was a must. During this course, my husband broke his leg and he was extremely demanding. I would visit him in the hospital in the morning before work, at my lunch hour and in the evening until late. I tried to bring my study materials to the hospital but I ended up failing. It was too much; the course was intense and the demands at home and dealing with his jealousy and insecurity was enough to break my focus. I was devastated. For the first time I was doing something for myself, and I blew it, I felt defeated.

My instructor approached me and offered me a deal. He said, "I understand that there is a lot going on at home. I'll give you the opportunity to have an incomplete instead of a fail if you will promise to retake the course the following semester." I jumped on it! It was my second chance. I was so excited to have the opportunity to make this right. During the remainder of the course, I was able to audit the class so that I would be fully prepared for the following semester. I found out later this was something the instructor offered to students who were eager and had a desire to get certified.

Throughout the process of auditing the class, I became the "patient". Once lectures were complete, the students would have to act out simulations of an emergency response. They had to put the skills they learned into action and I was their patient. I was put in the bushes so they had to get me out safely. I was laid on a stairwell. I even acted like a hostile drunk.

All of these things were extremely outside my comfort zone. I was scared, but at the same time elated. The students were so generous and kind to me for helping them that I was overwhelmed with joy. I felt like I was helping them and they were so grateful that I was. I had never experienced this before – human kindness, unconditional human kindness.

You see I had always been told never get too close to people because they ALWAYS want to take advantage of you or take something from you. So to see these people behave in a genuine and sweet way was something that lit a fire within me. I wanted more and more. I didn't want to leave. I couldn't wait for the end of the week to attend my Saturday class.

I always loved photography and videography so I created a picture slide and video with music for the students to see their growth and progress throughout the semester. When I showed it to them at the end of the semester, they were so grateful. They had all gathered money and purchased a gift card for me as a token of their appreciation. It may seem like a small token, but to me, it was everything. These people didn't have to do any of these things. They didn't have to hug me and thank me the way they did and it brought tears to my eyes and joy in my heart.

This act of human kindness was the catalyst for my desire to break free from the pain I was enduring in my home. I suddenly WANTED to LIVE! I wanted to feel this feeling of unconditional love; where you give love just to give it, and expect nothing in return, and then get more love back than you ever imagined. From that moment on, I chose life. That meant I had to get out of my current situation where death of my spirit was the only inevitable future. There was no going back, the line was crossed: it was over.

With all this said, there are some key areas to look at and steps to take to move you toward freedom of mind and spirit.

Step 1: Listen to your inner wisdom, your gut feeling, your intuition. One of the patterns of behaviour was to not trust myself. If you are uncomfortable, even for a moment, check in with that feeling. Ask: where in my body do I feel this. Separate it and observe it. Then ask yourself: what is that about? What is really going on here? Ask your inner feelings to speak the truth to you. It truly is your "inner knowing". It has all the answers for you. Connect with it, acknowledge it and seek it for guidance.

Step 2: You're brilliant, gorgeous and WORTH IT! No matter what experience you have had that has caused you to believe that you deserve anything other than complete and utter love and respect, know that YOU ARE WORTH IT! As you pick up the pieces of what is left of your life, and seek growth and learning, you will find out that you were beautiful and brilliant all along. Don't wait one moment longer! Know this NOW; don't let this be 20/20 hindsight. You are perfect and beautifully radiant and a precious soul to be cherished and loved, right now in this moment.

Believe that there is a fight in you bigger than you could have ever imagined. No matter how impossible the situation seems there is ALWAYS a way out. Sometimes when this is all the life we know, we can't see past our own experience. We believe that this is all there could ever be for us. I am living proof that there IS more! There is always help and always other options, but none of that will be of service to you if you don't own the belief first. You have to believe with every fibre in your being that anything is possible. Practice controlling the fearful voice that speaks so loudly in your head, limiting you from doing something, anything to get you out of your situation. Use the fear as fuel; let it be your guide not what keeps you a prisoner of the negative experience.

Step 3: Talk with someone. Share what you are feeling and what you are going through. Don't stay silent. My biggest pattern was shame. I lived in shame from the moment I had my first experience with my abuser. Shame was my "go to" for everything and since I learned to live by the inescapable family rule of "what will they say", I never spoke up to anyone. Two significant males in my life both told me that people wanted to sabotage a good thing so don't ever talk about anything that is going on at home. I believed them and played the role of living within the shadows their actions created in my life. No-one knew what I was going through. You are beautifully kind and friendly, share that with others, be YOU!

Step 4: Become the Powerful YOU that lives inside. Practise controlling the fearful voice that speaks so loudly in your head, limiting you from doing something, anything to get you out of your situation. Bring the powerful part of you to the forefront and calm the fear, use the fear as fuel, let it be your guide not what keeps you a prisoner of self doubt and shame.

My desire for this message is that you know that you can make your life what you want it to be. Nothing is impossible. You are smart, brilliant and never broken. You don't need to be fixed and nobody can take what you don't give them. Own your brilliance, own your power and own your radiance; once awakened, acknowledged and embraced, it is yours forever. You may share it and experience love within it and you will get more than you ever imagined, for when you own that fierce grace, so will everyone that you encounter.

Steps for your radiance to shine

Embrace life	- Find your purpose. - Take a second chance, keep your eyes open, second chances are offered. - Embrace life. - Love unconditionally and you will receive unconditional love.
Express gratitude	- Be thankful to others; show your gratitude to them – e.g. a thank you card. - You never know how your appreciation can change a person's life; this small gesture can make them feel valued and appreciated and be the catalyst for them to break free.
Listen to your inner wisdom	- Listen to your gut feeling, your intuition. - Trust yourself. - Check in with your feelings. - Ask: where in my body do I feel this and what is that about? - Ask your inner feelings to speak the truth to you and provide guidance.
You're brilliant, gorgeous and WORTH IT!	- You deserve love and respect; know that YOU ARE WORTH IT! - Don't wait one moment longer! - You are perfect and beautifully radiant and a precious soul to be cherished and loved, right now in this moment.
Seek growth and learning	- Through your growth you will find out that you were beautiful and brilliant all along

© Broken to Brilliant

Steps for your radiance to shine

There is ALWAYS a way out.	• No matter how impossible the situation seems there is ALWAYS a way out. • There IS more! There is always help and options, but none of that will be of service to you if you don't own the belief first. • Believe that anything is possible. • Practise controlling the fearful voice that speaks so loudly in your head. • Use the fear as fuel; allow it to guide you, not paralyse you.
Talk with someone	• Share what you are feeling and what you are going through. Don't stay silent. • Do not allow "shame" to silence you. • You are beautifully kind and friendly – share that with others, be YOU!
Own your radiance	• Make your life what you want it to be. Once awakened, acknowledged and embraced, it is yours forever. • Own your brilliance, own your power and own your radiance. • Share it and experience love within it and you will get more than you ever imagined.

Own your radiance, so that everyone you encounter will share in your brilliance.

© Broken to Brilliant

CHAPTER EIGHT

A JOURNEY OF SELF-DISCOVERY

"With confidence and love for yourself, I believe that you can achieve anything."

Funny, charming, cute, charismatic: four words I would use to describe him.

Drunk, loud, obnoxious and rude: four other words I would use to describe him.

I was in my early twenties when we met, recently returned from overseas and newly-single after leaving my long-term relationship. I was still trying to find my feet after travelling for so many years. Single for the first time in a long while, my self-esteem and confidence were quite low as I tried to find my way at home.

He came along and swept me off my feet. He was the cool, attractive, charismatic guy who seemed to have it all, and I was besotted by him. I had always felt like the cute, funny girl growing up, with a beautiful older sister and attractive friends. I was the one who was the best friend to all the guys, never the girlfriend. So when Mr Charismatic showed interest in me and we started dating, even when the cracks in his perfect veneer started to show, I just looked beyond it all. I felt lucky that a guy like him would even be interested in a girl like me!

He wowed me with an amazing date, picked me up in a limousine, whisked me off for a picturesque boat ride. I remember thinking, "Wow, this guy is really something special." Pulling out all the stops for that date was the first and last time he spoiled me.

It wasn't long until the cracks widened. Once again I chose to ignore them, blind to any imperfection that existed. He would often go out late with his mates, drinking and partying till the early hours of the morning, often not coming home for days on end. I would be beside myself with worry and so upset with him. He wouldn't or couldn't see that he had done anything wrong. My tears and anger at his selfishness didn't make him change his behaviour; it only made him angry and abusive towards me, as our fights would spiral out of control.

Often he made comments that put me down. Slowly, over time, this further eroded my self-confidence. He would rarely do anything for me or come anywhere with me, and I began to dread even asking him. When I did, it was like asking for the start of World War III. At first, there was no physical abuse. The emotional and mental abuse with his little comments here and there, going out with his mates, and the constant arguing undermined my self-confidence and my trust in him.

Finally, things got too much for me. After about five years of being together, and waiting in an empty bed for him to come home one too many times, I decided that was it, I'd had enough. I packed my bags and moved out.

However, he wouldn't leave me alone. He would ring me, message me, or come around to my house nearly every single day. After about eight months of not meeting anyone else and believing that maybe I'll never meet anyone else, I ended up getting back together with him. In hindsight it was probably one of the worst decisions I ever made, but isn't hindsight a beautiful thing? This time we lasted only about nine months. Things slowly went from bad to worse and it got to the point where we barely spoke to each other.

I used to describe him as Jekyll & Hyde, especially when he would drink. When he was drinking, I could tell when he was going to "click" from Dr Jekyll into Mr Hyde. It could happen at any time. I was constantly on my guard, not even able to relax when we were out for just a couple of drinks or for dinner with some friends and a glass of wine. If he got too drunk, "click": out would come horrible, nasty Mr Hyde. He would say dreadful things to me in front of family and friends with the sole purpose of embarrassing and upsetting me.

I remember one Friday night towards the end of our relationship; we had plans to go to a club with his friends. I didn't particularly want to go, but I hadn't been doing much with him and his friends. I thought that I really should go and try to show my support, even though I knew that our relationship was pretty much disintegrating before our eyes.

That night when I arrived home from work, he was with his mates, already drinking and well on his way to being drunk. I had a gut feeling that tonight was going to be one of those nights when Mr Hyde would return, and sure enough, it was. We arrived at the club and had only been there for 15 minutes. The first act had just started, the audience were all sitting down enjoying the show and Mr Hyde was emerging at the back near the bar, getting drunker by the second. For some reason he decided to come and sit next to me. He then proceeded to loudly and very rudely share how much he disliked the comedian. Embarrassed, I quietly but forcibly told him to be quiet and go away. Thankfully, Mr Hyde listened to me for once and left the table.

I had just started to relax and enjoy the show, when out of the corner of my eye I saw Mr Hyde heading into the corridor to go to the bathroom. Once again, something in my gut, some instinct, got me up out of my chair. I just knew something was going to happen. I grabbed my bag and raced after him. As I burst through the door into the corridor behind the bar, Mr Hyde was there, but he was not alone. A security guard had him by the throat, and he was yelling and screaming abuse at the guard. I didn't know what else to do but get between them. All I could think was that I had to get him outside the security door before anything happened. I pushed him slowly towards and finally out of the exit door. As soon as we were outside he turned his abuse onto me, calling me every name under the sun and saying the most horrible things. Turning my back on him, I left him in the car park hurling his abuse. I was done.

Thankfully I had only drunk non-alcoholic drinks so I could drive home. Somehow, he made his way home in the early hours of the morning, as I was woken by him knocking on the balcony door at five o'clock. I was still so upset from the night before that I couldn't even look at him, let alone talk to him. However, he wouldn't stop asking me questions like, "Why aren't you talking to me? What's going on? Why are you ignoring me?" As if I had done something wrong!

I looked at him with disgust. "You know this relationship is an absolute joke. What are we doing? I can't understand why we are even still together." With that, I turned and stormed out of the room. He hurled abuse as I walked away. I had to ignore him as I had a function on that day and needed to get ready to leave.

With my lack of response to his stream of abuse, he raged into the kitchen, his face bright red as he continued to scream at me. I wouldn't react, making him even angrier. As I turned my back to get something out of the cupboard, he picked up my breakfast bowl and threw it at my head. Just as he threw it though, I fortunately turned away. The bowl brushed past my ear and exploded against the wall. In shock, I turned and stared at him. I saw the back of his head as he stormed down the hall screaming and punching holes in the wall. I grabbed my things and left the house. The man I thought I knew and loved had tried to physically hurt me. I had no idea how I was meant to respond.

That night when I got home I apologised to him! Something in the back of my mind whispered, "You know, this is just like those ads you see about domestic violence. The man is abusive and the woman apologises for making him angry as if it is all her fault." I dismissed these thoughts though. How could an intelligent woman with her own business and seeming to be so together on the outside allow herself to be trapped in a domestic violence relationship?

Things seemed to get back to normal for about two weeks. However, the cracks were now the size of craters. On a Sunday afternoon after I'd been out for a hens' night and he had been out with his mates, we were meant to be sharing a quiet afternoon together. As usual we ended up doing what he wanted. Our quiet afternoon turned into an afternoon at his mate's place. Again I asked myself, "What am I doing?"

Finally the Universe gave me a sign that I could not ignore. It was Wednesday and I was heading out for my morning run, and as normal, I was putting my keys in the letterbox. As I looked in there, I noticed about eight small paper notes. As I read one, my heart sank and my stomach tied up in knots. I read the next one, and then the next. They were all exactly the same and they were all to my partner from a girl. Apparently they had met at the bar on the Saturday night he was out with his mates. She was trying to get in touch with him.

In shock, I turned and ran as hard as I could to try to clear my head. The only solution was to call her and find out for myself exactly what had happened. After speaking to the girl, it was finally the slap in the face that I needed. I didn't return home. Finally, our relationship was over.

I left that seven-year long relationship only a couple of months before my 30th birthday. My self-confidence was shattered but I knew deep within my heart it was the best decision I had ever made in my life.

I spent the next few years partying and looking for love with the wrong guys in the wrong places, often partying most weekends. My business was beginning to take its toll on me and my personal lifestyle wasn't making me feel any prouder about the person I was becoming.

It took a life-changing moment for me to make some big life

choices. I was confronted with a very close family member's crisis. I realised in an instant that if I didn't start asking for help and making some different decisions, I too could end up in hospital. Not long after that, I had three different episodes with three different girlfriends that made me wake up and realise that the partying and drunken nights out weren't making me feel good about myself. I really needed to make some changes in my life. It started with me stopping the drinking and partying.

Not long after that one of my girlfriends encouraged me to start doing triathlons, which I found I absolutely loved and became really passionate about. I started going to bed earlier on a Saturday night so I could get up and train with my triathlon squad the next morning. I made some fantastic new friends who were all passionate about being fit and healthy. My coach really motivated me to keep going all the time.

One of my best friends invited me to a personal development conference. There with many different speakers, promoting their different courses. I wasn't interested in most of them, however on the last day I was blown away by one phenomenal speaker. He described an intensive seminar and I knew I had to go. My best friend and I bought tickets and headed to the event. It was the most amazing, life-changing weekend of my life, the beginning of my personal development journey.

2014 was a year of self-discovery, attending the best workshops I have ever been to in my life, meeting the most amazing, inspirational people and learning so much more about myself. I realised that I could do so much more and I am worth so much more than I ever gave myself credit for.

One of the conferences was overseas where I shared a room with two amazing people who helped and encouraged me to push myself further than I had ever dared before. One of my roomies was also a single girl. We decided together that we were sick of being single and this was stopping us from doing the things we wanted to do. We made the decision together that we would start "going out on dates even if we didn't have anyone to go out with, and keep enjoying the outings we loved to do regardless of having a boyfriend". Before the end of the conference, we both sat down on the beach and wrote a list of every quality we wanted in a man and put it out to the Universe. Deep in my heart I knew that I was going to find him, so much so that I even made a commitment to myself that I would be in a committed relationship by February next year. It was December when I wrote that commitment.

I arrived home from the conference on a Thursday, and that very weekend a group of my friends had organized a skydiving adventure. I was still high and full of life after the conference, raving about how I was going to date myself, and my commitment to be in a relationship by February of the next year. Little did I know that an amazing guy was right there next to me in the plane, grinning and wishing me luck as my turn came to jump. As he grinned at me at 10,000 feet above the sea my life changed forever.

We started dating and seven months later, I knew deep in my heart that I had met my soul mate. He is the most caring and beautiful man. He takes care of me, showers me with love and affection, gives me support and joins me on all of my life adventures. I know that my journey of self-discovery and personal development helped to rebuild my confidence after the seven year relationship of abuse, and has lead me to my soul mate and my partner for life. With confidence and love for yourself, I believe that you can achieve anything.

Your journey to a new life

Don't miss these warning signs: "Love Bombing" – being wooed by overly romantic actions though admitting to a personal flaw, such as coming from a dysfunctional family.[11]

Do you:
- feel a loss of self-confidence?
- feel like you are walking on eggshells?
- avoid certain topics out of fear of angering your partner?

Does your partner:
- humiliate or yell at you?
- criticise you and put you down?
- blame you for their own abusive behaviour?
- treat you so badly that you're embarrassed in front of your friends or family?

Checklist for your journey to a new life

- Identify that you need to make a change.
- Decide what you really want – write a list!
- Undertake personal development.
- Attend self-development workshops or conferences.
- Make public your dreams and wishes.
- Stop negative behaviours eg drinking and partying.
- Start positive behaviours such as joining a group eg triathlon or Toastmasters.
- Make new friends with positive and healthy interests.
- Listen to your gut instincts.
- Look for warning signs and do not dismiss them.
- Don't go back.
- Surround yourself with positive and supportive people.

© Broken to Brilliant

CHAPTER NINE

MY WISH FOR HAPPINESS

"Life is about finding happiness."

THE MEMORIES HAVE FADED, ARE PUSHED AWAY, FORGOTTEN. I thought we were "normal". I thought it was normal that we did not mix with other people, that we had no car, that Nan was a pensioner and I had no brothers and sisters. That was all normal. It was all hidden. We had this cocoon and a rule:

"Don't you ever tell anybody anything outside of this house!"

It wasn't until I had my own children that I realised how far from normal my childhood truly was. The only photo I have of my infancy is a small black and white photo of me standing smiling in a dirt backyard with my grandmother. It is my only reminder that I was with my grandmother from a baby.

Initially, I was not sure if my story would be right for a book about how I got out of an abusive family and rebuilt my life. I thought that people might be confused, as I feel like the Lord saved me. He saw me from a long way away and pulled me out. Some people may think that this is a bit of Bible bashing and pooh-pooh it. However, a lot of people have and do relate to my story of success and happiness.

At 15, my mother was pregnant with me; she and my father had a shotgun wedding. For a couple of years they tried to make it work. I think my Mum was trying to find love she didn't get from her own mother. She eventually left me with her mother and went on to try to make her own life.

Alcohol was a big focus in the house every day and that meant my grandparents fought on a daily basis for as long as I can remember. I am sure my grandfather only stayed with Nan for me. I was not his biological grandchild, though he treated me like I was his own. I don't think his life was very happy.

My grandfather was the local publican. He would go to work at 5am to count the club money and then come home to take me to school. He worked every night and all weekend. It was a lonely life for Nan. Her best friend was the bottle. It stayed with her all the time to help drown her sense of loneliness and sadness.

Nan was not a happy drunk. She became violent and accusing. Each night as my grandfather got home at around 8.30 pm, she would be drunk and uncontrollable. She would fire insinuations that he had been having affairs. Nan would follow him around the house ranting lies at him. He did his best to ignore her. He walked away, but she kept coming at him, pestering, persisting with the insinuations until his only relief was to bash her.

I would stand between them trying to protect her, begging him to stop and leave her alone. Finally, the house would be quiet again. I remember clearly the "mornings after", watching her patting her black eye with make-up, trying desperately to hide her wounds and bruising. Then she would walk around the house and pick up the broken mirrors and other debris from the path of their rampage.

Life was hell for my grandfather too. Twice he left, but he always came back to take me to school. One of the worst times I remember, Nan was drunk by seven in the morning. As he returned home from counting the money at the club, he came up the stairs and she cracked the bowl of breakfast she had cooked for him over his head. He got a terrible fright, but then he was so angry it was terrifying. He threw some big punches into her that day.

Grandfather loved me, but he could not show me any affection. Sometimes when Nan got drunk she would come into my bedroom, lie next to me in bed and question me continually: "Has he been touching you?" She wouldn't leave me alone. No matter how many times I told her "NO" she just kept asking me and asking me. I would be lying there crying and hoping she would go away. Poor Grandfather; whatever he did, she was always suspicious. I felt so sorry for him. He deserved a better life. He used to suck on Quick Eze tablets; he always had indigestion. Eventually he died of stomach cancer. I knew he was unhappy, but I was too young to understand the chronic stress he was under.

Night after night I would cry myself to sleep, and pray that this would come to an end. Night after night I would stand between them begging them to leave each other alone, or I would be begging her to leave me alone.

Each day I went to school pretending nothing had happened. School was a relief. No-one knew or was suspicious. In fact, in primary school they didn't even know she was my grandmother. She looked and was young enough to be my mother.

Everyone else had a mother. I didn't want to be different. I always wanted a mother. Mum came to visit every now and then. I tried feverishly to get her approval. I tried everything, bribing her with whatever I had, even my favourite stuffed kangaroo-skin koala. It was a nice toy. Surely this would make her like me.

Eight years after I was born, Mum had another daughter, followed by a son. Nan never warmed to these two kids. During her continual drunken stupors, she reminded me how I had ruined her life having to raise a child at 40 years of age – how much better her life could have been without me. There was no chance Nan was going to be dumped with more kids again. The message was loud and clear: kids are an accident and an inconvenience.

Mum only came home when she was desperate or in between relationships. In her younger years she drank too much, then joined a support group, and married a man that she met there. This marriage had one condition: he would only take on one of her children. Overnight, my brother was taken from us and never seen again. It was like a murder. He disappeared, he was cut out of all the photos, it was like he never existed. He was never spoken of again.

Thirty-seven years later I'm still looking for my younger brother. I will never forget him and I often think about him. The problem is, in my mind I'm looking for a very cute, blonde two-year-old child. I have one photo of him. At first I was told he was adopted. Then I nursed his grandmother and she told me he was fostered out and had experienced a tough time. I hope not. One day, I hope I can find him. I feel that I could be of some benefit to him, now that my kids are grown. I could help him.

My mother's brief visits often ended in arguments with Nan about Mum being "dry" and Nan being "nothing but a drunk". Finally, Nan stopped drinking. Our house was for a while a happy one. Nan did love me. She even took me to Disney on Ice, we went to the movies and she would cook nice meals for me.

I remember very clearly the day we worked in the yard all day. Nan said she had worked so hard that she deserved just one drink. And then it started where it had left off. The yelling demons and violence filled our house and our lives again. It all came back worse than ever. It was like a vicious demon, it took over our house and our lives.

When I was in Grade 9, my grandfather had a stroke and they carried him away on an ambulance stretcher. We took two buses to go to visit him in hospital, and he would cry all the time. I would shave his face and read to him. I feel bad that his life was so miserable. He stayed for me and I didn't get to say thanks. I have many things I would have liked to say to my grandfather, but mostly I would have liked to have been old enough to say "thanks". Thanks for staying, thanks for caring for me, thanks for driving me to school.

By the time I was in Grade 11, Nan had deteriorated significantly. Her drinking got worse. She no longer slept in a bed; she slept on the couch. In the middle of the night she would scream out to me, "Turn off that bloody radio. If you don't, I'm going to kill ya!"

I used to be scared of her bashing me, but the roles were reversing. She was becoming weaker and I was becoming stronger. As I came into my teens I was becoming stronger and fitter. Taking up Jujitsu and Judo helped. Nan had continually threatened me, leaving me cowering before her, but I didn't feel so threatened by her any more. Her health was deteriorating. She didn't eat, she only drank and vomited. I still remember the smell.

I was too young to realise she was going through the DTs (delirium tremens). As her alcoholism progressed, her body and mind deteriorated. Eventually she was unable to walk and unable to eat. She lay on the couch and vomited. She stank. I went to school. Still no-one knew. I started to notice I was getting headaches on the way home. Years later, I realised it was the subconscious tension about what I was going to find when I got home. I sometimes worried, "If she dies, who will look after me? Where will I go? Will I end up in an orphanage?" Nan had often reminded me how lucky I was to have her, that if it wasn't for her, I would have gone to an orphanage.

In the end, I was disgusted with my Nan. I did my own thing. I would shut the bedroom door and do my homework. I had a pseudo life, at school and in my bedroom. I had school, neighbours and church.

One day, I needed Nan to sign a form for me to go on camp. She was collapsed on the floor. She tried really hard to focus to sign the form. I told her when I left for school I would ring the doctor. I don't remember how I rang the doctor. When I got home, she was gone. She never came home again. What was I going to do?

A friend from church took me up to the hospital to visit Nan. She lay in the hospital bed, trembling and shaking with the DTs and horrors. She was only 55 years old. Eventually she was locked up in a mental institution. They had never seen an alcoholic as bad as her and in all my years of nursing, I have never seen an alcoholic as advanced as her.

One day at school Mum arrived. She was smiling. "I've come to look after you," she said. I wasn't sure. Where had she been all my life? Did she really want to "look after me"? After a little while, Mum thought it would be good for me to meet my father. I was 17 and had never met him. It was a strange meeting; we didn't know what to say to each other, so it was mostly small talk. I liked the fact that finally I found someone who looked like me. I wanted to call him "Dad" but I just couldn't as he hadn't been a dad to me. I liked him. He seemed more interested in my mother than me, and before long he was gone again.

Mum and I tried to make it work, but she was only 15 years older than I was. I didn't really want her telling me what to do. We tried and failed. Eventually the fighting started to remind me of Nan and my grandfather. I told Mum I would leave the house; I was thinking this would help put a permanent roof over my sister's head, as she had been moved around all her life. If I left, there would be no more fighting. Maybe my sister could finally have some stability in her life. She and Mum would be happy in Nan's house. My mother's response was, "That is the best news I've ever heard. You've always wanted a mother; you will never have one. I am only your mother by birth. Go!"

She took over our family home. I didn't own a suitcase and

wasn't allowed to use cardboard boxes from under the house, so I rode my bike down to the local shopping centre to get boxes to carry my few worldly possessions.

I stayed with a friend up the road until I started nursing. At least I would have a roof over my head at the nurses' quarters. Life would be better there.

My Plan: Saving, planning, education, church and support got me out of where I was

Growing up, I lived on granny smith apples and cooked myself processed cheese on toast and locked myself in my room. I started my own little ecosystem of hiding in my room, trying to do really well so I could get out of there. I remember that even in Grade 1, I was completely focused on how I was going to escape. I knew it meant I would have to save my money. So I saved my $1 a week pocket money to get a car. A car would carry me away. It was my only way out. Later, when I had a part-time job, I saved every cent. A car would be my gateway to freedom. I had to get out!

I also knew I needed an education, so I focused on my homework. Good marks would get me out of this hell. Being very determined, and trying to combat being an average student, I worked really hard and had a strong work ethic. Anything I didn't understand, I would be knocking on the teacher's door and getting them to help me. The teachers kind of liked that, and it had a few advantages as they would go the extra mile to help me. There were certain teachers that understood me and were very kind to me, but they never knew what was going on at home.

It was important for me to be fit and strong so that I could protect myself from Nan, so being a community recreation leader was a natural career choice. However, this career choice didn't provide accommodation. It had to be nursing. Nursing provided somewhere to live at the nurses' quarters and an instant humble income.

Lucky for me the neighbours were great. They had no idea of the life I lived over the fence. I spent most of my time there. They weren't allowed over to my house. They didn't know Nan was drunk most of the time. I stayed over there as long as I could each day, returning home at dark. We played all sorts of games: hopscotch, murder in the dark and tennis. The days were fun there. Whenever the weeds grew and the dandelions would dry, I would pick them. We had one each. We all made a wish. "Normal" kids wished for a new bike; I always secretly wished for happiness. Surely this life would get better one day.

When I was 14 I went to a church concert, which I really liked. At church, people cared for me. They took me in. I felt accepted and useful. The Lord was looking down and he grabbed me and picked me up. That was the turning point in my life. I got really involved in church; I kept going there and really enjoyed it. It gave me some guidelines and hope; it showed me what "normal" was. I felt like I found the happiness that I had been wishing for in the dandelions.

Sometimes people would have me to stay at their house for the weekend. They would buy scorched almond bars, and take me on trips into the city where we would eat gelato. I remember all that – it was really special. I asked myself,

"Is this what normal people do?" They accepted me! They also worked on some of my attitudes, the aggressive attitudes. Gently they would say, "You need to think about that." One woman who was single would take me to a youth group, and then drive me home to my grandmother's house. I would never want to go back in the house, so I would try to distract and stall her so we could talk until midnight in the car. We became good friends.

I feel that throughout my life the Lord has always put the right people in my path at the right time. When my grandmother was put in hospital, a friend's mother down the road offered to take me in; I could sleep at their house at night.

At the hospital the nurse in charge said, "What are you going to do? Well, you're headed for the streets." She saw my dysfunctional family and thought I didn't stand a chance. A year later, as I came down the hill at the hospital in my new white cap and starched uniform, she recognised me. She said, "OH my goodness. I thought you would be on the streets as a prostitute." She was very happy her prediction hadn't come true.

The church is still a strong part of my life. I give to my church because it supports the local community, a boys' home, people who are in hospital with no friends or support, single mothers, and it helps those people who cannot manage their yards anymore. It is for people who need to feel loved. I love that it is a place for people to feel safe and recover, and they don't have to get trapped in abuse. It is really quite amazing. I know the Lord personally; for me it is something in your heart not in a book. I feel very privileged that the Lord saw me from far away and pulled me out. My faith has kept me strong and stayed with me.

As I look back, I can see that through my life I have helped others. By seeing my life's experience as a lesson I have continued to be able to help others. Even when I was at school I would see people who were lonely. They had no friends, they also did not belong and there they sat alone in the library. So, I would go to the library and invite them out. Years later, I met one of those girls. We were in our late 40s. She said, "You know, when you invited me to the local shopping centre, at that time I thought I had finally made it in life." To remember this event 25 years later shows the significance and lasting impact of how we treat others.

People just need a friend. I am very happy I am in a position to be able to continue to help others. A real priority for me is keeping the group called the Stray Birds going and making people feel good about themselves. It is about connecting people. Many of the members are women who have gone through a divorce and lost friends. One of the good things about Stray Birds is that they all feel loved and accepted, and we are achieving things such as going for bushwalks. It's a group of great women doing great things. Having fun is our motto, and providing a feeling of acceptance and achievement. One of the members said, "In my darkest days of divorce, I feel fantastic."

You do not realise how much is buried. I have had to get rid of the hardness and I am still recognising the hardness. My husband told me, "You don't have to have your dukes up all the time." I had no affection growing up. I never wanted to sit next to anyone or be close to people, there had to be a space in the seat next to me in church. Now, I can sit closer to people and I have learned to give hugs, though I am not as affectionate as most women. I was used to: "If you come home without shoes on your feet I will smash you until your nose bleeds."

All I want is for my children and my grandchildren to know they are wanted, they belong, and they are loved. I was always the unwanted child. My grandmother didn't want me, and my mother still doesn't want me. When I would visit my mother, that's all I was: the visitor. Even my father didn't want me. That is how it was with me – no-one wanted me. I didn't belong.

The unwanted child goes on for generations. My children don't have a grandmother who wants them, they don't have cousins, nor uncles or aunts. The Scripture says that the sins of the forefathers run through the veins of the family for three generations.

> *"The Lord...visits the iniquity of the fathers on the children and the children's children, to the third and the fourth generation." (Exodus 34:6-7; Deuteronomy 5:8-10)*

I think we have now gone past the three generations – my grandmother, my mother and me. I was the last in my line of unwanted children. I have never felt resentful about my life. So many people have suffered, in so many different ways and had so many things to deal with. The Lord saved me and gave me hope.

My life is rich and full. I love nursing. I met my husband – he is a very good man. I now have three wonderful adult children. I have amazing friends and good health. I still don't see my mother – she still doesn't want me. My father sees me once every five years. He still doesn't know what to do with me. My faith has kept me strong and stayed with me.

I am thankful for my life experiences. It has made me who I am. These experiences have enabled me to understand other people's misfortunes. The key is to have a vision. There is a scripture that says "where there is no vision, the people perish" (Proverbs 29:18). So you need to be really focused, to have a plan, seek out Faith, become educated and save your money to assist the transition. Also learn to love unconditionally and stay hopeful. The Lord saw me from far away and gave me life. I am very thankful for all that I have.

I am thankful every day that I am fit and healthy. Nursing experiences show you many tragic stories of people whose lives are cut short. I have continued to work on my fitness and have taken up cycling. I love it. It is a great chance to get the wind in your face and see the best of each day, meet amazing people and feel great by achieving new little goals. I am privileged to be so healthy and be surrounded by amazing, inspiring people.

My friends, husband and children, you are the happiness I wished for. I have great people around me: family, friends and workmates. I meet so many amazing people and there is incredible respect for each other. I have a life filled with happiness and I am truly thankful.

Life is good. Life is rich when you are surrounded by amazing people. Watching people achieve goals and support each other brings fantastic happiness.

Life is about finding happiness in each other and the simple things in life, achieving small goals and celebrating every one of them with great friends.

For that I am eternally grateful.

By the way, I'm not a writer. When Broken to Brilliant asked me to write this chapter, I was quite overwhelmed. This chapter was something I've always wanted to do and didn't know how. Thanks to Broken to Brilliant for helping me share my story. It was hard to relive it, but telling it has been healing. It has also helped me reflect and feel thankful for my happy life.

I hope you get something out of my story and your life is blessed. Never Miss an Opportunity!

May you also have everlasting happiness and achieve great things in your life, whatever that may be, great and small.

Try my SPECS to help you achieve happiness

Saving

- Save your money to assist the transition. Saving got me out of where I was.
- Save money, be consistent even it is $1 a week. Make it a habit – this will help to take you to freedom.

Planning

- Have a plan and a vision. There is a scripture that says "where there is no vision, the people perish" (Proverbs 29:18).
- Take up a group sporting activity e.g. cycling, Jujitsu.
- Stay fit and healthy.
- Stay really focused and be very determined.
- Never miss an opportunity.

Education

- You need an education – work hard and have a strong work ethic.
- Stop and reflect on how amazing life is.
- Be truly thankful.
- Learn to love unconditionally.
- Stay hopeful.
- Be thankful for your life experiences and see your life's experience as a lesson.

© Broken to Brilliant

Try my SPECS to help you achieve happiness

- Be kind – how we treat each other has a significant and lasting impact.
- Never feel resentful about your life. So many people have suffered so much more.

Church

- Seek out Faith. Turn to the Lord – this was my turning point in my life.
- Join a church you really like. People make you feel loved there. They will take you in, make you feel accepted and useful.
- Give to your church because it supports others in need.
- Get involved in the church, it will give you guidelines and hope.

Support

- Surround yourself with amazing and inspiring people.
- Seek help from others, like good neighbours.
- Help others.

CHAPTER TEN

WE ALL NEED A SLICE OF SPAM

*"Why keep going? Why stands for **W**hat **H**eightens
You to go out and take action against the odds."*

WE HAVE ALL HEARD OF SPAM – YOU KNOW, THE HAM IN A CAN type of SPAM, not the electronic kind. Many of us may have tasted SPAM, some may like it and some may not. But this is a story is about how SPAM can make a difference.

My childhood memories are filled with lots of businesses and spending time at the country races, popping on a few bets and going out for Chinese dinner if there was a win. When settling down, I dreamed about how idyllic our family life would be: love, romance, and two close families working for business success, sharing Sunday lunches, enjoying family card games and parties, going to fancy restaurants and enjoying family holidays. Life would be wonderful as our families had gotten on and done these things together for many years.

I did not want to be the "brown jug left on the shelf". So settling down with a man who made a few bets was no big deal – or so I thought! But basically I made some big mistakes. The first, we were both on the relationship rebound, and the second thinking a few bets were no big deal!

Gambling overtook our lives. He stole and hocked items, fleeced bank accounts, and in just one day, lost over $20,000 at the casino. The gambling escalated, he lost more and more money and as his desperation increased, so did the abuse.

I remember the fear and the torments: killing is easy, look at these knife skills, do you know how many types of pet mince there are, who would suspect foul play if someone drowned as they were caught on a snag in the river.

At the bottom of my cup I would find residue, and I would lose time. Unfortunately, I found out what had happened during those lost hours.

Before a significant family event, I chose to end the relationship; false confidence or having back up? I am not sure but enough was enough. That night under the cover of a loud party next door, my child and I found ourselves locked in the house, the phones were unplugged, I awoke with a pillow being pushed firmly over my face, kicking and screaming, breaking free, my screams for help drowned by the thumping party beats next door. Then a rope was placed around my neck and I received the reassurance that I had "brought this upon myself". I don't know how I did it, but I wrestled free, pushing my screaming child in front of me, somehow we got the keys and burst through the front door, there was a lot of commotion and then we disappeared into the darkness, behind bushes and the neighbour's fence.

It didn't end there. We pretended our lives were normal going to work and school but living in fear. When the pets died we knew we could not stay and we needed a refuge. The legal wrangle was torturous and dragged on; eventually we had permission to leave. I drove us across the country to safety and to start our new life.

As a jobless, homeless, single mum, I arrived at a family member's best friend's home. They kindly interrupted their lives and allowed us to live with them in one room for five months. We each had one small suitcase.

You would think that would have been enough to deal with. In those five months we had to deal with a lot more. The very system that was meant to support us created a whole swag of roadblocks. At first I could not get single parent benefits as they did not believe me. No-one would rent a house to a single mum with two kids and two dogs. All our furniture was lost because the removalist company had been sold and the new company could not find my furniture. When they did find it and they shipped it, they rang me to say that the train had rolled over and they did not think it would be in a good state of repair.

The children were booked into schools next to each other. We arrived for the interview at one school where a place had been promised only to find it had been forgotten and our place at the school no longer existed. The children ended up at schools hours apart from each other. There was mostly nil or very minimal child support, not that I ever expected it anyway. I weighed 47 kg and had aged ten years in one year. I only had a part-time job. Could it get any worse?

That was me! Let me tell you how low I really was: I didn't believe I was of enough value to live. While I was living in that abusive marriage, one day as the police responded to the seriousness of the incidents, the detective phoned me and was yelling at me to get out of the house. I was yelling at him, "I don't care if I die. If I die then everyone will know the truth."

You may be asking "Why?" Why did I keep going? For me I think Why stands for What Heightens You to go out and take action against the odds. My two kids are my WHY. They deserved to be safe, to have a great education. I had to undo what I had led them into; I had to set them on a better course in life.

What got me out of there? SPAM got me out and it all started with **Support**. I received support from the community services organisations, my family, the police, close friends, my boss, work colleagues, the refuge workers and Community Law Organisations. Without this support I would not be here today.

I may have been out, but I was angry – angry at the world. I felt betrayed by people who knew things that I did not know, like the years of infidelity: there was so much going on behind my back. Why didn't people tell me? There were plenty of people to blame, to be angry and frustrated at for the position I was in. In the quiet of night, while the kids slept, I would uncontrollably sob. I didn't show my anger to many people, just my family. But my family couldn't deal with my expressions of disappointment and betrayal. We nearly become estranged.

My attitude was not great. I knew in my heart that there was a better way, there was more to life. I had to give back to my kids and make their life great and undo all that hurt. I was hurting and I was very negative. So I searched for the answers. I read lots of books about domestic violence, how to raise boys and girls. I listened to audios and DVDs and enrolled in self-improvement and business development courses. I rarely watched television.

There was a turning point for me and my attitude; there were two key things that helped me to begin to look at things differently.

The first turning point occurred during the five months we stayed at our friend's home. She said to me, "How do you keep going, when so much more stuff just keeps coming?" And then she gave me a book by Norman Vincent Peale, *The Power of Positive Thinking*.

The first chapter starts with **Believe in yourself! Have faith in your abilities.** He provided a prescription to treat terrible disbelief in yourself – rules to overcome inadequacy of attitude:

- Picture yourself succeeding; cancel negative thoughts.
- Ten times a day repeat these words: "I can do all things through Christ which strengthens me."
- Get a competent counsellor.
- Make a list of all your values – everything you are grateful for.

I wrote my list of all that I was grateful for in a small spiral bound book. I repeated the words "I can do all things through Christ which strengthens me", and read my list and said these words during the one-hour train commute every day. The tears streamed down my face but I read it, said it (under my breath), read it and said it. And I attended domestic violence counselling. That book got me on a roll!

The second turning point came when the kids worked at a video shop and they brought home a DVD with a genie on the front cover for movie night. We settled with popcorn and lollies, but just after the beginning, the kids did not want to watch the movie as it was about one law – the secret is the law of attraction.

This video said: everything that is coming into your life you are attracting into your life. Hang on! I did not attract the gambling, the debt and abuse! The next line in this movie was:

> *"I am here to be in your face and say yes you did attract it! It's the hardest concept to get but once you have accepted it, it is life-transforming."*

How was all the abuse, infidelity and gambling my fault? That video went back with the instructions to the kids: do not get that out again! However, a year later they borrowed the same DVD without realising it. I knew then that I had to watch it again and this time, I got it! The book and the DVD helped to get me back to being a positive person. Being **P**ositive is the P in SPAM; it means persist until you are thinking positively.

The lessons of positive thinking from the book and the Secret became part of my daily routine. With renewed enthusiasm, I rewrote my list of what I appreciated and I had to take action and be grateful for everything I had every day.

My list was large; I wrote it on an A3 sized sticky note and put it on the wall near my bed. I said thank you every day before getting out of bed and before going to sleep. This wasn't easy; the old habits of noticing everything bad with the world would creep back. I found that by going to bed reading positive books, I would wake up more positive. If the first thing you think about is the things you appreciate, you start the day positively.

Taking **A**ction is important. I needed to make things happen, find the solution, find some help. I tried not to wallow as the tears rolled. Instead I cleaned or cooked and kept taking action. I got an audio version of the Secret and kept playing it for about two years.

Having to restart was hard and money was tight. Money may not be everything but you can do a lot more and help a lot more people with it than you can without it. My parents were not poor but every cent they had, they worked hard for, and so they deserved the money they had. From them, very early in life, I learned that you had to work for money. I worked in the family business before and after school. As a youngster, I made and sold decorated cakes to my mum's friends. At school, I taught aerobics classes and cut kids hair or pierced their ears, and sold my school lunch order. At university, I washed taxis at 2.00 am in the morning to make money.

If I needed money it was up to me to make it. I never had any money problems while I was single. I could save and budget my money. Despite my husband's extreme gambling, I still managed to make ends meet and stretch every dollar further than you would think it could go. I tried really hard to teach my kids how to make money and how to manage money – I had to. They trusted me with their money and they still do. I taught my kids to allocate money for what they wanted by using the envelope method. Growing up, I watched a television show on how to manage your money by dividing it into velvet moneybags. I taught the kids to manage their money by dividing it into envelopes. My daughter remembers using the envelopes to save for her pink skate shoes and my son remembers saving for his console games. They saved and reaped the reward of purchasing what they wanted. They learned how to make money through lemonade stands, selling second hand toys, doing chores for friends and neighbours. They also learned the importance of the balance sheet, the marketing plan and saving money for what you want.

My tip is: you do not mess around with money. You need to take action, before the debt collector knocks on your door. Go stop your hocked valuables from being on-sold. Ring up the electricity company and negotiate a bill extension. Ask for help. I asked family to help put a roof over our heads and they did. We will forever be grateful that they invested in our house. I have also routinely set aside time every week to pay bills and work out my money. I created a system to help me manage my money and I have learned to allocate money to areas such as bills, fun, education – and to stick to it. You have to monitor your money and revise the plan.

Have you ever wondered why the bills just keep coming and they rack up to thousands? It is because they are regular, consistent and persistent. They do not stop. If you apply the same principal of being regular, consistent, and persistent and pay yourself first, then you will see your savings stack up or your credit cards paid off.

I have used this approach with paying the private school fees, house renovations and now paying for my education courses. I was the best at managing my money when I had less of it!

Most people could not work out how a single mum, who was not getting much child support ($20 per month), could send her kids to independent schools and on all the excursions. It was because I budgeted my butt off and I was frugal.

So what does support, positive thinking, appreciation, action and money management have to do with SPAM? I did not believe I was worthwhile or of enough value to live. I thought that being killed would send a bigger message. I just wanted people to know the truth of what happening to us. The only way I thought that I could be of value was to die to reveal this truth.

Fortunately, people were supporting me and they kept on supporting me. Family rallied around, we stayed with family and friends, people rang me every day to make sure we were all okay, they came and sat with us, my boss at work made sure I turned up every day. Also people we did not know helped us. Those people are the ones who support charity groups; they donate food, money and clothing.

The story of SPAM began before we left. It was Christmas and we were in a cockroach-infested refuge. I had already had to move out of my home as it was so unsafe. My boss had given me a beautiful flower arrangement to make the refuge look nice.

I had been advised to stay in the refuge but I could not face Christmas there. As we were cleaning our unit, a big white laundry basket full of Christmas food was delivered to us. It was so full we could hardly lift it. I could not believe that people who did not even know us were giving us this wonderful food hamper. That basket was packed into my little silver car. Its contents helped to feed us as I drove the kids across the outback. I had to be careful about spending money now I was homeless and jobless.

We bought some fresh bread, sat at a picnic table, and ate SPAM and tomato sauce sandwiches. Those sandwiches tasted soooo good. The kids wanted to know why we had not eaten SPAM before. About five months later when we had moved into our new home, the kids felt like SPAM sandwiches. So we sat at the lounge room table, with cardboard boxes as curtains in the windows. I bought fresh baked bread and made SPAM sandwiches. They were shocked. With voices of surprise, they said:

> "You've bought the wrong SPAM! This isn't what we ate in the outback; it doesn't taste as fantastic."

It didn't and it never will. Those SPAM sandwiches eaten at the dusty park bench in the middle of the outback had a secret ingredient. That SPAM was infused with the love and support of people who cared. People cared enough which helped us survive.

SPAM stands for the four key things that have helped me to overcome lots of adversities and challenges and turn adversity to advantage and rebuild our lives. These are:

- **S**upport
- **P**ersistent and **P**ositive thinking
- **A**ppreciation and **A**ction
- **M**oney management

My kids and I are living proof that kindness, support and SPAM can make you feel like you are worthwhile and valued. Our lives have turned around, we have a roof over our heads, cars to drive and we are becoming financially sound.

Today, our lives are more than we could have imagined. Being a part of helping other women and their children rebuild their lives following domestic violence is one step in the grand plan of beginning to help others.

> *"There is very little difference in people, but that little difference makes a big difference. The little difference is attitude."*
> *~ W. Clement Stone*

Open your own can of SPAM to help get you back on your feet

Support	- To help you get through this traumatic time and rebuild your life, you will need different types of support from different people and organisations. - First you will need to ask for help. - Identify the areas that you need support e.g. emotional, financial. - Join a support group. - Find and book in to see a counsellor. - Find one confidant that you can laugh and cry with.
Persistent and **P**ositive thinking	- Picture yourself succeeding. - Cancel negative thoughts and words. - Ten times a day repeat these words: "I can do all things through Christ which strengthens me." - Persist on being positive until it becomes a habit. - Read books, take workshops, work with a counsellor/mentor/life coach/Transformologist™ to change your attitude.
Appreciation and **A**ction	- Write a list of what you are grateful for. The purpose of this process is to connect and really feel thankful for what you have; this is not a grocery list or another item on your to-do list. - Feelings of gratitude and really connecting and appreciating what you truly have is required. At first this may not be easy to see but it takes practice. - Take action, be grateful, read and re-write your list every day, morning and night. - Take action to deal with things that are coming your way. A head-in-the-sand approach will not solve anything: take action, address it, make a decision.

© Broken to Brilliant

Open your own can of SPAM to help get you back on your feet

Money management	• You need to make your own money – be financially independent, work for your money, retrain yourself. • Allocate your money to categories such as bills, fun, education. • Use a tool like electronic bank accounts, a written budget, an application or a spreadsheet, to allocate your weekly or fortnightly money. • Plan time once a week to monitor and review your budget. • Ask for bill extensions early, develop payment plans if necessary.

© Broken to Brilliant

GLOSSARY

THE WOMEN IN THIS BOOK HAVE EXPERIENCED MANY FORMS OF ongoing abuse. This glossary provides definitions for domestic and family violence and the associated behaviours.

Domestic and family violence, also known as domestic violence, family violence, partner violence or intimate partner violence, is a pattern of abusive behaviour between family members and/or intimate partners, usually, though not exclusively, taking place in the home, that over time puts one person in a position of power over another, and causes fear. It is often referred to as a pattern of coercion and control. Abusers are sometimes called "perpetrators of violence". [12, 13, 14, 15]

Family and domestic violence is any violent, threatening, coercive or controlling behaviour that occurs in current or past family, domestic or intimate relationships. This includes not only physical injury but direct or indirect threats, sexual assault, emotional and psychological torment, economic control, damage to property, social isolation and any behaviour which causes a person to live in fear or torment.[12, 13, 14, 15]

Types of abusive behaviour associated with domestic and family violence are listed below:
- Physical abuse – including direct assaults on the body (shaking, slapping, pushing), use of weapons, driving dangerously, destruction of property, abuse of pets in front

of family members, assault of children, locking the victim out of the house, and sleep deprivation.
- Sexual abuse – any form of forced sex or sexual degradation, such as sexual activity without consent, causing pain during sex, assaulting genitals, coercive sex without protection against pregnancy or sexually transmitted disease, making the victim perform sexual acts unwillingly, criticising, or using sexually degrading insults.
- Emotional abuse – blaming the victim for all problems in the relationship, constantly comparing the victim with others to undermine self-esteem and self-worth, sporadic sulking, withdrawing all interest and engagement (e.g. weeks of silence), blackmail.
- Domestic violence threats are a form of emotional abuse and are threats made within the context of an abusive relationship. Whether the threats are of a physical, sexual or emotional nature, they are all designed to further control the victim by instilling fear and ensuring compliance.
- Verbal abuse – continual "put downs" and humiliation, either privately or publicly, with attacks following clear themes that focus on intelligence, sexuality, body image and capacity as a parent and spouse or capable person.
- Social abuse – systematic isolation from family and friends through techniques such as ongoing rudeness to family and friends, moving to locations where the victim knows nobody, and forbidding or physically preventing the victim from going out and meeting people.
- Economic abuse – complete control of all monies, no access

to bank accounts, providing only an inadequate "allowance", using any wages earned by the victim for household expenses.
- Spiritual abuse – denying access to ceremonies, land or family, preventing religious observance, forcing victims to do things against their beliefs, denigration of cultural background, or using religious teachings or cultural tradition as a reason for violence.

The above behaviours are from Box 1.1: Behaviours associated with domestic and family violence, Office for Women 2008; Inspire Foundation 2008.

CONTACT NUMBERS

Australia National

- 1800 RESPECT (1800 737 732)
  24 hour, National Sexual Assault, Family & Domestic Violence Counselling Line for any Australian who has experienced, or is at risk of, family and domestic violence and/or sexual assault.
- Lifeline 131 114
  National number who can help put you in contact with a crisis service in your State (24 hours).
- Police or Ambulance
  Dial 000 in an emergency for police or ambulance.
- Translating and Interpreting Service 131 450
  Phone to gain access to an interpreter in your own language (free).
- Mensline Australia 1300 78 99 78
  Supports men and boys who are dealing with family and relationship difficulties.
- Kids Help Line 1800 551 800
  Telephone counselling for children and young people.
  E-mail and web counselling www.kidshelp.com.au.
- Australian Childhood Foundation
  1800-176-453 or 9874-3922
  Counselling for children and young people affected by abuse
  www.childhood.org.au or www.stopchildabuse.com.au.

Broken to Brilliant—149

- Relationships Australia
  1300-364-277 or Vic (03) 9261-8700
  Support groups and counselling on relationships, and for abusive and abused partners.
  Website: www.relationships.com.au
- ASCA (Adults Surviving Child Abuse) 1300 657 380
  A service to adult survivors, their friends and family and the health care professionals who support them.
  Support line: www.asca.org.au
- National Disability Abuse and Neglect Hotline
  1800 880 052
  An Australia-wide telephone hotline for reporting abuse and neglect of people with disability.
  www.disabilityhotline.org
- LGBTIQ Domestic Violence Information
  Another Closet: www.anothercloset.com.au
- Transgender and Transsexual People
  Gender Centre (02) 9569 2366
  Services for people with gender issues.
  www.gendercentre.org.au

Australian Capital Territory
- Domestic Violence Crisis Service (02) 6280 0900
- Rape Crisis Centre (24 Hours) (02) 6247 2525
- Canberra Men's Centre (02) 6230 6999
- Legal Aid ACT 1300 654 314

New South Wales
- Domestic Violence Line 1800 65 64 63

1800 671 442 TTY (Hearing impaired)
- Rape Crisis Service 1800 424 017
- Interrelate Family Centres 1300 736 966
- LawAccess NSW 1300 888 529

Northern Territory
- Domestic Violence Crisis Line 1800 019 116
- Sexual Assault Referral Centre (08) 8922 6472
- Northern Territory Legal Aid Commission 1800 019 343

Queensland
- Domestic Violence Telephone Service 1800 811 811
- Sexual Assault Help Line 1800 010 120
- Men's Info Line 1800 600 636
- QLD DV WebLink
  A directory of QLD support services.
  www.qlddomesticviolencelink.org.au/
- Legal Aid Queensland 1300 65 11 88

South Australia
- Domestic Violence Helpline 1300 782 200
- Yarrow Place Sexual Assault Service 1800 817 421
- Legal Help Line 1300 366 424

Tasmania
- Family Violence Counselling and Support Service 1800 608 122
- Family Violence Response & Referral 1800 633 937
- Sexual Assault Support Service (03) 6231 1817

- Mens Line Australia 1300 364 277
- Legal Aid Tasmania 1300 366 611

Victoria
- Safe steps Family Violence Response Centre 1800 015 188 or (03) 9322 3555
- Sexual Assault Crisis Line 1800 806 292
- Men's Referral Service 1800 065 973
- Victoria Legal Aid 1300 792 387

Western Australia
- Women's Domestic Violence Helpline (08) 9223 1188/ 1800 007 339
- Crisis Care 1800 199 008 or (08) 9233 1111
- Sexual Assault Resource Centre (08) 9340 1828 or 1800 199 888
- Men's Helpline (08) 9223 1199 or 1800 000 599
- Legal Aid WA 1300 650 579

United States of America
- The National Domestic Hotline 1-800-799-7233 | 1-800-787-3224 (TTY)
- National Suicide Prevention Lifeline 1-800-273-8255

United Kingdom
- National Domestic Helpline 0808 2000 247 24-hour National Domestic Violence Freephone Helpline

Contact details were correct at the time of publication.

ENDNOTES

1   Evans, D. 2007. "Battle-scars:Long-term effects of prior domestic violence," Centre for Women's Studies and Gender Research, Melbourne.

2   Tually S, Faulkner D, Cutler C and Slatter M. 2008. "Women, Domestic and Family Violence and Homelessness: A Synthesis Report." Office for Women and Inspire Foundation. Flinders Institute for Housing, Urban and Regional Research Flinders University http://www.dpmc.gov.au/women/publications-articles/safety-women/women-synthesis-report-HTML.cfm#c

3   Department for Planning and Community Development, *Family violence risk assessment and risk management framework*, Victorian Government, Melbourne, 2007, p. 21. http://www.dhs.vic.gov.au/__data/assets/pdf_file/0006/581757/risk-assessment-risk-management-framework-2007.pdf

4   National Council to Reduce Violence against Women and Children (NCRVWC), Background paper to "Time for Action: The National Council's plan to reduce violence against women and children", 2009–2021, Department of Families, Housing, Community Services and Indigenous Affairs (FaHCSIA), Canberra, 2009, p. 13. https://www.dss.gov.au/our-responsibilities/women/publications-articles/reducing-violence/national-plan-to-reduce-violence-against-women-and-their-children/background-paper-to-time-for-action-the-national-

councils-plan-for-australia-to-reduce-violence-against-women-and-their?HTML

5   World Health Organization 2012. Information Sheet: *Understanding and addressing violence against women Overview.* WHO/RHR/12.35 http://apps.who.int/iris/bitstream/10665/77433/1/WHO_RHR_12.35_eng.pdf

6   The Foundation to Prevent Violence Against Women and their Children and Australian National Research Organisation for Women's Safety (ANROWS). *Violence against women: key statistics.* http://www.anrows.org.au/sites/default/files/Violence-Against-Australian-Women-Key-Statistics.pdf

7   Queensland Government Special Taskforce on Domestic and Family Violence in Queensland; Queensland Government. About the Taskforce. https://www.qld.gov.au/community/getting-support-health-social-issue/about-dfv-taskforce/

8   State of Queensland (Queensland Health), October, 2015. StatBite #69 Hospitalisations for Domestic Assault, Queensland, 2005-06 to 2014-15. Health Statistics Unit Queensland Health, Brisbane. https://www.health.qld.gov.au/hsu/pdf/statbite/statbite69.pdf

9   Victorian Health Promotion Foundation. September 2014. Australians' attitudes to violence against women 2013 *National Community Attitudes Towards Violence Against Women Survey – Research Summary.* Publication Number: P-MW-184. https://www.vichealth.vic.gov.au/media-and-resources/publications/2013-national-community-attitudes-towards-violence-against-women-survey

10   Scott, K. 2015. MX News "Domestic violence an act

of 'Romantic Terrorism'" http://www.mx.net.au/domestic-violence-an-act-of-romantic-terrorism/c269011793dcb05daa0bc-4c5f59fb996/ Book refered to in the article. Hayes S and Jeffries S 2015, *Romantic Terrorism: An Auto-Ethnography of Domestic Violence, Victimization and Survival.*

11   Krug EG et al., eds. 2002. *World report on violence and health: summary.* World Health Organization, Geneva. http://www.who.int/violence_injury_prevention/violence/world_report/en/summary_en.pdf

12   The Women's Council for Domestic and Family Violence Services (WCDFVS) 2011. "What is Domestic and Family Violence?" http://www.womenscouncil.com.au/what-is-domestic--family-violence.html

13   Department of Health & Human Services (DHHS). 2011. "What is family violence?" State Government of Victoria   http://www.dhs.vic.gov.au/for-individuals/children,-families-and-young-people/family-violence/what-is-family-violence

14   Office for Women Department of Families, Housing, Community Services and Indigenous Affairs. 2008. "Behaviours associated with domestic and family violence" sourced from *Women, Domestic and Family Violence and Homelessness: A Synthesis Report.* Box 1.1 Flinders Institute for Housing, Urban and Regional Research. https://www.dss.gov.au/sites/default/files/documents/05_2012/synthesis_report2008.pdf

www.ingramcontent.com/pod-product-compliance
Lightning Source LLC
Chambersburg PA
CBHW070618300426
44113CB00010B/1581